Root Cause Analysis in Developmental Disabilities

Understand Why Bad Things Happen

How to Use Root Cause Analysis to Prevent Adverse Events in
Developmental Disabilities Service Organizations

Steven D. Staugaitis, Ph.D.

University of Massachusetts Medical School
Center for Developmental Disabilities Evaluation and Research

DEDICATION

This book and the entire *Risk Management in DD* series is dedicated to all the people who happen to have an intellectual disability and who are striving to experience acceptance, dignity and respect in their daily lives.

CONTENTS

ACKNOWLEDGMENTS

This book is part of a series entitled **Risk Management in DD** and is designed to accompany the *Root Cause Analysis* course that is available in the online internet-based suite of educational courses available at the University of Massachusetts Medical School's udiscovering.org website. The online courses, in addition to the content contained in the series books, present a number of additional resources including video-based and interactive learning tools that can enhance the educational experience. Both the books and online courses in this series have been specifically designed for personnel who work with and support individuals with intellectual and developmental disabilities within the public and the private service sector, as well as those who have responsibility for monitoring and evaluating these services and supports.

Much of the material contained in this book as well as the entire **Risk Management in DD** series is the result of careful review of national and international practice standards and is based on extensive hands-on experience working within the field of developmental disabilities service by the author. The content that is included in this book and the approach to risk management that is presented throughout the series is therefore both evidence based and practical. Perhaps of equal importance it is designed for direct application and use by I/DD service providers and systems. Taken together the series represents a "toolbox" for the mitigation of risk and enhancement of quality in services and supports to people with a disability.

The **Risk Management in DD** series of on–line courses was developed with the support of a federal grant from the National Institutes of Health.

NIH Grant Number 5 R42 HD063179-03

FOR MORE INFORMATION
about the **Risk Management in DD** series please visit our website at

http://www.udiscovering.org/

TO LEARN MORE ABOUT THE ON-LINE COURSES
in the **Risk Management in DD** series go to Chapter 1 in this book
or
TO ACCESS THE ON-LINE COURSES GO TO
http://www.udiscovering.org/products/risk-management-developmental-disabilities

Thank you
Steve Staugaitis

ABOUT THE AUTHOR

Steven D. Staugaitis, Ph.D.

Dr. Steven Staugaitis is on the faculty of the University of Massachusetts Medical School, Department of Family Medicine and Community Health where he provides support to the E.K. Shriver Center, Center for Developmental Disabilities Evaluation and Research. Steve has over 40 years of direct experience working with individuals with intellectual and developmental disabilities and in administering local, regional and statewide programs and services. He is a licensed clinical psychologist who has managed large I/DD facilities and regional support systems serving people with disabilities. Steve has been a consultant to a variety of state and private provider I/DD organizations within the United States, providing technical assistance, training and support in the areas of risk management, program and systems evaluation and quality assurance and improvement. He has been a principal investigator on a number of federal grants, including a grant from the National Institutes of Health (#5 R42 HD063179-03) that supported the development of the series or on-line courses: *Risk Management in DD*.

CHAPTER 1

An Introduction to Risk Management in DD

Special Note: Chapters 1 and 2 are presented in each of the books and on-line courses in the *Risk Management in DD* series. The first chapter summarizes the course content across the entire series. The material contained in the second chapter (Culture of Safety) represents an important foundation for understanding the complex issues that so often contribute to the adverse events that can result in serious harm and even avoidable death for people with a disability. Understanding these issues is absolutely essential for the enhancement of safety in I/DD services. It is a necessary condition for properly managing risk and improving quality in the I/DD service system. If you have already read this material in one of the other books or courses please skip forward to Chapter 3; or better yet, simply re-review the material in Chapter 2 that you are most interested in.

BAD THINGS HAPPEN. Unfortunately, they seem to happen way too often to people with intellectual and other developmental disabilities. They happen in poor programs and services, they happen in mediocre programs and even in the best programs. Bad things happen when people choose and control their own supports and the people who assist them. Bad things happen even when staff are well screened, trained and supervised. They happen despite managers and advocates reminding everyone to be "vigilant" and to "pay attention." Bad things happen. They happen even though the vast majority of staff are caring and well intentioned people - trying their best to do a very challenging job.

Why is it that "bad things" continue to happen in programs and services that support people with intellectual and developmental disabilities, even though "everyone" talks about the importance of safety and quality? And despite expensive and sophisticated monitoring, incident reporting and quality review systems - and requirements and mandates and regulations - that try to "manage" quality and safety in just about every DD agency and state across the nation?

Is it inevitable that "bad things" will happen in service systems that have become overly complex? Or, are there perhaps some basic and underlying factors that, if recognized and aggressively addressed, could make a difference? A big difference.

It has happened in other fields when there has been a concerted effort to reduce risk — for example, most recently in acute healthcare. Why can't it happen here - in the field of developmental disabilities?

Well it can! This series of books and on-line courses is designed to help do just that. By choosing to learn more about improving safety and reducing risk of harm you are demonstrating your interest and commitment to make a big difference in the quality of your supports and in the life of the people you serve. So, welcome to the Risk Management in DD series.

THE RISK MANAGEMENT IN DD SERIES

THE FULL SERIES includes six detailed on-line courses and accompanying books that provide useful tools for enhancing your ability to design and establish effective methods for reducing adverse events and improving the safety of services for people with intellectual and developmental disabilities (I/DD). The on-line courses include a number of audio-visual and interactive learning tools as well as downloadable forms and checklists, many of which can be filled out on-line. The accompanying books are useful as stand-alone resources or can be used to supplement the on-line experience.

All of the courses and books in this series have been specially designed to provide practical knowledge and skills for a broad range of personnel in the field of intellectual and developmental disability services (I/DD). This includes individuals who are responsible for conducting activities such as individual support planning, the coordination and supervision of services and supports, and/or the monitoring and oversight of programs and service systems that support people with I/DD in service provider and public/state systems of support and oversight. All of the books and courses include practical tools that you can use right away, including interactive forms, checklists and resources. Taken together the series represents a comprehensive risk management "toolbox" that can be used to reduce risk of harm and improve the safety and quality of services and supports to individuals who have a disability. The full series includes:

1. **MORTALITY REVIEW AND REPORTING IN DD: How to Use Mortality Review and Reporting as a Quality Enhancement Tool.** The Mortality Review and Reporting in DD resource provides information about methods for conducting mortality reviews within organizations and public agencies that serve persons with developmental disabilities. Methods for establishing review processes and analyzing and reporting findings are highlighted that are consistent with generally accepted standards for mortality review. Content includes step by step directions along with a variety of forms and checklists for setting up, managing and reporting on your mortality review process, including major findings. Information regarding simple methods to analyze mortality

2

data and establish comparative benchmarks and improvement goals are presented.

2. **RISK SCREENING IN DD: How to Use Risk Screening to Enhance Individual Support Planning.** The Risk Screening in I/DD resource provides information on and skill development directed toward understanding some of the most important issues that pose special risks for persons with I/DD. It guides the development and design of protocols for screening risks and integrating results into individualized support plans. Issues associated with special considerations for addressing planning needs for self-directed support models are included.

3. **ROOT CAUSE ANALYSIS IN DD: How to Use Root Cause Analysis to Prevent Adverse Events.** The Root Cause Analysis in DD resource provides introductory information on managing risk and enhancing safety in programs that serve people with I/DD. It includes step-by-step instructions for using the process of root cause analysis in the field of I/DD. Worksheets, checklists and other tools you can use are included.

4. **FAILURE MODE AND EFFECTS ANALYSIS IN DD: How to Use FMEA to Promote Safety.** The Failure Mode and Effects Analysis in DD resource provides background information and practical step-by-step instructions for using failure mode and effects analysis (FMEA) as a risk prevention tool in programs serving individuals with developmental disabilities. FMEA is a recognized method for conducting prospective review of complex processes and activities in order to identify and correct steps that have a perceived high risk of error. In this series the FMEA process is adapted to the types of issues and adverse events most common within programs and settings serving persons with developmental disabilities. Forms and other tools are included in the material along with practical examples from I/DD programs you can use to better understand how to introduce FMEA to your service system.

5. **USING DATA AS A QUALITY TOOL IN DD: How to Use Data to Promote Quality Improvement.** The Data Analysis for Quality Improvement course and associated book is designed to provide basic skills in analyzing risk and quality improvement related data. The focus of instruction is on using descriptive and inferential statistical procedures to help identify patterns and trends that may be associated with increased risk of harm, including client characteristics and environmental variables. Practical examples, templates and resources are included.

6. **INCIDENT MANAGEMENT IN DD: How to Use Information and Data as an Incident Prevention Tool.** The Incident Management in DD resource provides information on standards for establishing and enhancing existing incident reporting, review and management systems for I/DD agencies. Material includes a review of the most common incident categories that are typically present in incident management systems, methods to evaluate the usability, comprehensiveness and potential effectiveness of incident reporting

systems and instruction on how to integrate findings into a more holistic risk management system. This includes the development of "triggers" for highlighting high risk situations. Checklists and other practical tools are presented.

An additional book supplement is available that is entitled **SYSTEMS DESIGN IN DD: How to Use a Comprehensive System for Risk Management.** This supplement includes information on how to "pull together" all of the various risk management tools in order to design a more comprehensive systems approach to safety and quality improvement in the field of intellectual and developmental disabilities. This supplemental material is included in each of the on-line courses and as a booklet entitled **Systems Design in DD**. Readers interested in designing and evaluating their overall approach to risk management are encouraged to review this supplemental material.

To access the suite of on-line courses in this series
visit the following internet site:

http://www.udiscovering.org/

and select the link for

Risk Management in Developmental Disabilities

CHAPTER 2

Getting Started:
Create a Meaningful Culture of Safety

THE FOUNDATION FOR ENHANCING SAFETY in any I/DD organization requires the presence of an organizational culture that expects everyone to focus on safe practices and promote quality in every single aspect of their work. Assuring the presence of such a vibrant organizational culture of safety is the single most important component of any risk management system. Without this foundation, efforts to ensure safety and minimize unnecessary risk to the people that are supported by an organization will be severely compromised if not impossible to achieve. Pay careful attention to it!

A culture of safety requires a strong commitment on the part of every person within the organization to think differently about safety. Beginning with senior leadership and extending outward to all stakeholders, a clear and consistent vision must be firmly embraced that represents a different "way of doing business." Direct support personnel, service providers and recipients, family members, supervisors, managers, advisory boards - literally everyone involved in the organization must see safety as essential to the delivery of quality services. They must incorporate safe practices into all of their daily activities. All members of the organization must believe that safety is essential and that they can each play an important role in making it happen – all the time. It is this organizational commitment and belief, embodied in the attitudes and behavior of its members that is meant by the concept culture of safety. Such an organizational culture is the single most important aspect for building a strong foundation for safety and quality.

A SAFE AND INFORMED CULTURE IS CRITICAL. The British psychologist James Reason[1] has addressed the importance of creating a *safe culture* by focusing on understanding important barriers that inhibit safe practices and that can interfere with the establishment of an organization-wide culture of safety. First and foremost Reason emphasizes that "an informed culture is a safe culture."[2] He notes that such a culture is embodied by a belief in the importance of a *systems* approach that continually gathers and analyzes information. A systems approach actively seeks out information that can help identify weaknesses in the system that can lead to harm - and areas where safety nets and policies are working as intended. According to Reason, an organization that has an informed and safe culture seeks constant, informed improvement and establishes an atmosphere where people are comfortable sharing mishaps and mistakes. In such an organization staff know that their leadership recognizes that most people do not deliberately try to cause harm. The members of such an organization believe that it is only through open and honest reporting and tough analysis that the real *causes* of risks can be understood and effective changes can then be made to improve safety.

David Marx[3] has expanded on this idea by introducing the construct of a *just culture*. In a just culture, there is a sense of fairness and openness. Managers in a just culture do not automatically blame people for mistakes, but rather look to use adverse events as learning opportunities. They seek to manage choices and redesign systems to reduce the likelihood of human error. In an organization with a just culture consequences for harmful incidents are based on an understanding of why errors may have taken place. The focus is therefore on understanding, not blaming.

Marx identifies three basic causes of adverse events that should be recognized and then addressed differently to improve the safety of the tasks and activities that are typically performed by personnel.

1. **Human error**, which is not intentional and is due to a mistake, a slip or a lapse;

2. **At-risk behavior**, which is intentional but is due to a lack of awareness of the risk, or, is due to a belief that the risk was justified in order to achieve a desired outcome; and,

3. **Reckless behavior**, which is a conscious and deliberate disregard for the risks involved.

As suggested by Marx, it is extremely important to understand the difference between these three causes of adverse events and to establish different methods of remediation and correction based on the actual cause. Unfortunately, the typical management response – using discipline and punitive consequences – may be appropriate for adverse events known to be due to reckless behavior, but it is counterproductive when such incidents are caused by actions that are unintentional (error) or where the risk was not recognized. In these instances different responses and solutions are needed.

MISTAKES HAPPEN. Sometimes people make mistakes. But when a genuine culture of safety is present within an organization, there is a shared understanding that everyone can and sometimes does make a mistake. In fact, both Marx and Reason recognize that mistakes can be valuable "lessons" and opportunities for improvement. In the health care field, it is becoming more and more recognized that "bad systems and not bad people lead to most errors."[4] This important notion is illustrated in a quote by Donald Norman[5] that is shared by Marx:

> *People make errors, which lead to accidents. Accidents lead to deaths. The standard solution is to blame the people involved. If we find out who made the errors and punish them, we solve the problem, right? Wrong. The problem is seldom the fault of an individual; it is the fault of the system. Change the people without changing the system and the problems will continue.*

Recognition of the importance of an organizational culture of safety is as important in I/DD as it is in health care and virtually every other field of endeavor. Establishing such a culture is the very first step – and an essential ingredient - for safe services that can meet the highest standards of quality in the field of I/DD.

HOW TO CREATE A STRONGER CULTURE OF SAFETY

HOW CAN YOU PROMOTE a stronger culture of safety within an I/DD organization? One of the most important first steps is to assess the organizational culture that currently exists in the organization. Think about what steps can be taken, on both a short term and longer term basis, to help establish a more positive and safe culture. You can use the checklist in **Appendix A** to guide such an evaluation and planning process. Involve others in the assessment to the extent possible.

Next, explore the extent to which the organization embodies important principles and practices that promote a meaningful culture of safety. Remember that effective and meaningful management of risk requires the involvement of everyone within a service organization. Pay special attention to the following practices.

STOP BLAMING. An I/DD organization with a true culture of safety creates a climate of support where staff are not fearful of retribution or punishment if they make an honest mistake or identify a problem. Rather, they feel supported by their managers and leadership within the organization to correct problems and point out issues that may jeopardize the health and safety of the people they serve - and of one another. A fear of punishment and retaliation is a powerful barrier to identifying and reporting adverse events and errors. When an atmosphere of distrust and fear is present, it is difficult, if not impossible to establish an effective culture of safety. Therefore stress the need to change attitudes and beliefs (especially for managers and supervisors) and move away from "blaming" and toward "understanding." The organizational climate has to become one that encourages identification of issues in order to ascertain what needs to be changed and improved rather than focusing on who is to blame.

MAKE REPORTING CONFIDENTIAL. Experts in the field of safety (e.g., Reason) believe that open reporting can be better established when an organization sets up processes that maintain the confidentiality or "de-identification of reporters." They suggest that it is better to establish separation within the agency (or part of the agency) so that the entity that collects incident reports is different from the agency (or part of the agency) that handles discipline.

INVOLVE EVERYONE. An organization that is truly committed to safety seeks out and reinforces the active involvement of front-line staff and service recipients. It works hard to facilitate honest and open communication between staff, persons receiving supports, their families and advocates, and the leadership of the organization. Such an organization recognizes that the people closest to the problem are very often in the best position to identify it and provide practical solutions.

BE A LEARNING ORGANIZATION. In order to establish a culture that rewards safety it is important to promote constant learning. To do this, leaders should strive to make their agency a "learning organization" – one that uses information from outside their immediate system to better understand the causes of adverse

7

events and potential solutions to problems. In other words, work to become an organization that actively seeks the experiences of other industries and other agencies to help target processes and systems that can be improved. As noted by some experts (e.g., Marx), an adverse event should not be seen as simply something to be fixed, but also something to learn from. An organization that has a firm foundation of safety doesn't let "good enough be good enough," but rather it consistently seeks opportunities to gather information for improvement - from all stakeholders - at all levels of the organization – and especially from outside of the organization.

STRIVE TO UNDERSTAND WHY. Perhaps most importantly, an organization with a well-established culture of safety always attempts to look beyond "fault" and tries to understand <u>why</u> an error took place. This drive for understanding is essential. It represents a mind-set that is deeply engrained in the organization and shared by everyone. It is a belief that we must understand not only what happened, but why it happened. Only then can an effective plan for lasting change become a reality. Such an organization moves beyond a focus on blame and punishment - which addresses only the immediate event. An organization with a functioning culture of safety strives to implement systemic change - improvements in procedures and protocols - in how business is done. In other words it seeks changes and improvements that can actually reduce the risk of harm to the people it supports and to bring about long-term positive change; not simply implement changes that "look good."

UNDERSTAND THE ROLE OF HUMAN ERROR

RECOGNIZING THE CRITICAL ROLE OF HUMAN ERROR in causing adverse events is necessary for creating a safe environment for people with disabilities. Almost all services and supports that are provided to persons with intellectual or developmental disabilities are labor intensive, i.e., they require people – usually staff, volunteers or family members – to conduct a task or activity with and on behalf of the person with the disability. Sometimes these tasks are rather complex and therefore prone to errors. Before effective risk prevention strategies can be established, it is necessary to identify what type of error led to an adverse event. Efforts to correct problems or prevent future incidents will fail if there is not an understanding of why something went wrong. The enhancement of safety, management of risk and promotion of quality demand that you and your organizational leadership recognize and understand the role of human error.

DIFFERENTIATE THE DIFFERENT KINDS OF HUMAN ERRORS. As noted above, it is important to recognize that not all human errors are the same. For example, Patricia Spath[6] has categorized errors that take place in health care settings such as hospitals using a classification that can be readily applied to I/DD services. A simple adaptation to this method for categorizing errors results in a classification of errors as either *active* or *latent*. When you go about analyzing adverse events and the potential for risk of harm to people in your program and/or service think carefully these two major types of errors and how they have contributed to the incident under study.

ACTIVE ERRORS are human errors that are usually committed by a person or group of people, most often front-line direct support personnel who are working with the individual with a disability. These types of error are the most "noticeable" and are usually associated with the proximate cause of an adverse event, i.e., they take place immediately before the incident. There are three major types of active errors that can take place:

- **Slips** – these are *unintentional deviations* from an established procedure, often due to distraction or inadequate attention to the task at hand. Very often the person making the error forgets to do something or does it at the wrong time. For example, consider a staff member who, while preparing an individual for transfer using a mechanical lift, is interrupted and asked a series of questions about how to conduct the program for another person. The staff member fails to properly attach the restraining strap on the first person who subsequently falls and injures himself.

- **Mistakes** – these are often due to *faulty reasoning* and poor judgment. They are not intentional and are often associated with a novel or new situation or even when supporting an individual the staff member may not be familiar with. Mistakes that take place when performing a more complex activity have a high probability of resulting in an adverse event. For example, consider the situation where a staff member is directed to supervise an individual they have never supported before due to the regular person calling in sick. The new staff member provides the individual with paper materials that are part of an activity they often conduct with other service recipients. However, the new staff member is not aware that the consumer has a history of impulsive behavior and pica. The service recipient tears the paper and begins to ingest it, and then begins to choke. This was a mistake (not intentional) related to lack of familiarity with the person they were supporting.

- **Unsafe practices** – these errors are associated with an *intentional* or *conscious decision* to do something "risky." Unsafe practices are almost always a direct violation of rules and/or standards. They often take place when a staff member is "rushed" or makes a deliberate decision to take a "short cut" in order to save time or make a difficult task easier. Sometimes the unsafe practice can even take place as a function of staff convenience. For example, consider this: a staff member leaves a person temporarily alone in a van in order to "run into a store" because there is no parking nearby and getting the service recipient to cooperate with exiting and entering the van will take a lot of time and effort. The staff member is aware that the individual has a history of running away when unsupervised, but they decide that the risk is "worth it" since they will be gone only for a few minutes. When the staff member is in the store, the service recipient leaves the van and runs into the street where she is hit by a car. The intentional act by the staff member led to the adverse incident.

LATENT FAULTS are errors or faults in *system design* that serve to set the stage for active errors. They are usually the responsibility of management. Latent faults increase the probability that a slip, mistake or unsafe practice will occur at some time in the future. Latent faults usually have the following characteristics:

- **Delayed impact** – the fault or system design failure is usually *not immediately evident* and often goes unrecognized. It is identified only after one or more significant adverse events have taken place that result in an analysis of the system as a whole.

- **Set the stage for failure** – latent faults are most often present early in the "chain of events" that leads up to an adverse event. They *set the stage* for later errors by staff. Latent faults are often associated with confusing policy and procedure, inadequate training, scheduling issues (e.g., multiple activities at the same time) or staff shortages, punitive work environments that lead to stress, and fear of failure, and conflicting priorities and unrealistic expectations.

A careful analysis of most serious adverse events will be able to identify the presence of BOTH active errors and latent faults. Whenever you are designing a program, developing an individual support plan, reviewing protocols or conducting a retrospective or prospective hazard analysis make sure you consider the entire "chain" of possible events that could cause an adverse event to take place. Work backwards from the most obvious or proximate cause of the incident to uncover those system design factors that set the stage for active errors by staff. A failure to do this will most likely result in an incomplete understanding of what led up to and therefore contributed to the adverse event. This will result in you "solving" the wrong problem and thus increase the probability that in the future the same type of adverse event will take place.

REVIEW THE ENTIRE ERROR CHAIN. A more complete understanding of what has caused and/or contributed to an adverse event therefore requires you to carefully review the full sequence of events that preceded the incident. All too often only the actions and errors associated with direct support personnel are reviewed during incident investigations. This results in a tendency to focus on "corrective" actions such as retraining and staff discipline that will not address the underlying problem that led to the human error in the first place. Meaningful corrective actions will only take place when management makes an effort to identify latent faults in the system that set the stage for staff errors. If a particular type of adverse event occurs over and over again, it is imperative that you take the time to carefully review the entire error chain. Effective management of risk can only <u>prevent</u> future incidents when it targets underlying systems faults.

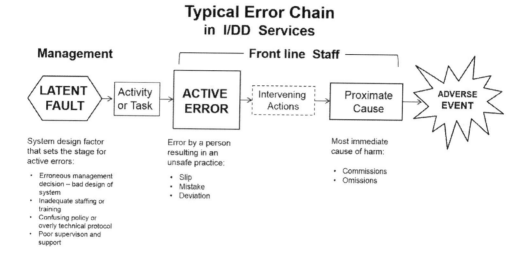

PROGRAM VARIABLES THAT INCREASE ERROR.

THERE ARE A NUMBER of important and somewhat unique characteristics of services and supports to individuals with an intellectual and/or other developmental disability that can increase the risk of error by support providers. Some of the more important risk factors that can promote error in the I/DD field include:

1. **VARIABILITY.** The risk of human error is directly related to the degree of variability or the difference in the needs and characteristics of the people being served and the people who provide the support. It is also related to differences that exist in the routines, activities and types of settings within which those supports are provided. The greater the variability, the greater the risk an error will occur.

   a. **People.** Unlike many other service organizations and industries, the people served by I/DD systems typically span a very broad range of capabilities and therefore have substantial variability in individual needs and preferences. This broad difference in needs and preferences requires the introduction of highly individualized and unique services. Such "people variability" is present due to a wide range of:

      i. Physical capabilities and physical disabilities

      ii. Intellectual capacity

      iii. Behavioral health and challenges and the need for unique behavior support and intervention plans

        iv. Medical co-morbidities and the need for specialized health-related care

    b. **Staff.** Unlike medical services and acute healthcare (*as well as many other professional service industries*) there are currently no recognized national credentialing, standards or professional criteria for direct support personnel in the field of I/DD in the United States. Therefore, it is not unusual for the individuals who provide care and support to persons with disabilities to also exhibit significant variability in their skills and ability to deliver consistent and often complicated care related services. This is especially true now that self-directed support using person-selected support assistants has become more widely utilized. Such staff variability is illustrated by differences in staff:

        i. Educational background and training

        ii. Knowledge and experience

        iii. Skills and competency

        iv. Language proficiencies and culture

    c. **Services.** Given the wide range of needs within the population typically served by most I/DD programs, the types of services and individualized supports that are provided vary significantly, and cover a very expansive range, including supports related to:

        i. Residential living

        ii. Special education and employment

        iii. Community access and leisure activities

        iv. Transportation

        v. Health care and nursing related care

        vi. Behavior management

        vii. Physical mobility, communication and adapted technology

Even within any given category of support there is even greater variability (e.g., supervised living, independent living, group homes, foster care, institutional care, etc. just for the one category referred to as *residential* living). The same types of differences exist in all of the other major support and service categories. Such variability is essential for assuring there is a focus on individualized supports that can better meet personal needs and preferences. But, with such variability comes increased risk of human error that should be recognized when designing systems of support.

2. **COMPLEXITY.** The more complex a task or activity, the higher the risk of error. The delivery of services in the field of I/DD has become increasingly more complex over the years. The sophistication and complexity of the

activities staff are called upon to perform raises the probability that errors will be made. This important relationship between task complexity and error has been studied more extensively in the field of healthcare than in the field of I/DD. However, since many of the issues between the two fields of practice are extremely similar, we can extrapolate many of the findings and projections. For instance, The Institute for Healthcare Improvement[7] suggests that the number of steps in any activity performed by healthcare workers – despite the inherent reliability of each individual step - is directly related to the probability an error will occur. For example, if a task has 25 steps, and the reliability of each step is 99%, the task will be completed without any error only 78% of the time. This means that there is a 22% chance an error will occur each time the activity or task is undertaken! Many of the individual programs and the tasks that staff are called upon to conduct with persons who have more significant disabilities have at least 25 to 50 separate steps. Many tasks have steps that must be performed in a particular sequence and in response to subtle cues and individual reactions of the person receiving support. This translates into a relatively high probability that errors will occur.

It is therefore highly likely that some type of human error will take place in most complex processes or activities performed by staff who work in I/DD services. Fortunately however, most errors do not necessarily lead to serious adverse events – at least not to incidents that cause severe harm. Unfortunately, many of the tasks that direct support personnel serving people with severe disabilities are asked to perform on a regular basis are extremely complex. Consequently they are therefore very prone to errors taking place. Those errors can – over time - have very negative consequences, including severe injury and sometimes even accidental death. Just think about the total number of complex tasks that are performed every day in your organization and you can begin to recognize that the potential for human error is enormous.

Consider the following examples of complex activities that are typically performed in I/DD programs that are prone to increased risk of error and resultant injury or death:

- **Mealtime and eating.** Preparing special diets and implementing specialized feeding programs for persons with significant swallowing disorders.

- **Behavior.** Implementing complex behavior management programs, sometimes including the use of physical contact and restraint, with persons who are resistive, confused and aggressive.

- **Medication.** Administering multiple medications, some of which are extremely potent and must be maintained within a relatively narrow therapeutic range.

- **Bathing.** Assuring that persons with very limited muscle control are safe and comfortable when participating in special bathing procedures.

- **Transportation.** Properly implementing lift and transfer protocols for persons with mobility disabilities and providing proper support and management of persons at risk of aggressive behavior and/or running when being transported.

3. **COUPLING.** Coupling is a concept that refers to the extent to which discrete steps in an activity follow each other in rapid succession. The less time there is between steps, the greater the degree of coupling. Tightly coupled tasks are associated with increased error since there is little, if any time to recognize mistakes and take corrective action before the next step in the activity must be implemented. Tightly coupled tasks are therefore more prone to progressive errors. For example, if a particular step is not performed correctly it may become difficult, if not impossible, to perform the next step correctly. If there is no time delay between these steps, the errors cascade (i.e., one error quickly contributes to the next and to the next, and so on). This error progression provides little or no opportunity to stop or interrupt the process in time to prevent harm from taking place.

There are many different types of "tightly coupled" tasks or activities in I/DD programs. A few of the more common activities include:

a. **Restraint.** When staff implement a physical restraint or other physical management technique with an individual who is highly agitated it can require very fast responses on the part of the staff, with little time to "think through" or correct minor mistakes in how they are applying the restraint and responding to the person. This can quickly lead to mistakes and resulting injury to the individual and even the staff.

b. **Feeding.** Providing food and nourishment to an individual who has a significant swallowing disorder and who may be restless and/or resistant (e.g., moving and shaking their head) can often require quick reactions on the part of staff as they move through the sequential steps of the feeding procedure. Even minor errors in feeding someone with a swallowing disorder can lead to choking and the potential for aspiration.

c. **Lift and transfer.** Assisting an individual with limited motor control very often requires almost instantaneous responses and corrective reactions on the part of staff, particularly if the individual resists physical support. The lack of time between sequential steps in this type of activity can lead to progressive errors that can result in "accidental" falls and severe injury.

4. **LIMITED STANDARDIZATION.** Standardization usually increases the probability that certain tasks or activities will be performed the same way, every time and by every staff person. Such standardization reduces error and the resultant risk of an adverse event. That is why many industries (e.g., aviation, nuclear engineering, industrial manufacturing, and medical surgery) spend significant time and resources on evaluating procedures and developing formal protocols that require

the use of standardized procedures and formal checklists that must be strictly adhered to by personnel.

The movement in the field of I/DD toward "individualization" and "person-centered" approaches to care and support that reflect personal preferences and needs has undoubtedly promoted great improvement in the quality of life and quality of service for the persons with disabilities. These trends have also made it more difficult to standardize programs, services, procedures and the myriad tasks that staff are asked to perform every day. Consequently, those who are responsible for designing and managing programs and services must recognize that many care and support procedures will not be conducted the same way every time they are carried out by staff and therefore more prone to human error.

In addition to the "individual" focus present within I/DD services, a number of other factors may also operate to reduce the standardization of procedures. Some of these include:

- **Lack of familiarity with people and routines.** Long term retention of direct support professionals is a special challenge for many service providers due to the demands of the work and pay and benefits that may not be competitive. This can lead to frequent turnover of personnel. Staffing requirements can also lead to personnel being "pulled" from one program setting to another to ensure adequate coverage. Both of these factors tend to compromise the ability of staff to become familiar with the individual needs and communication styles of the people they support and the special (and often complicated) individualized programs that must be provided to each individual. This lack of familiarity with people and routines can heighten the risk for mistakes and errors that can cause harm.

- **Multiple providers.** Different service providers may be present for an individual's residential versus employment related supports. Different service providers often have different methods and procedures, not to mention, different support staff that interact with individuals with a disability. This makes standardization of tasks and activities extremely difficult if not impossible across providers, even when specific protocols are present. The result is an increased risk of human error.

- **Dispersed services.** The I/DD service system has made remarkable progress in helping people live and work within a more integrated and community-based support system. People live semi-independently or in very small group residences. They work in individualized jobs with varying degrees of intermittent support. This major change in how services are delivered has resulted in a highly distributed support system where staff often work alone or with a very small number of colleagues. The presence of direct supervision and direction is often not available. The reduction in direct supervision and the limited presence of other staff to answer questions, discover mistakes before they cause any harm, and provide assistance can increase the risk of error. In addition, programs and service settings may, even for a single provider, be quite geographically distant from one another, resulting in differences in supervision and management expectations and methods. Certainly this doesn't mean small settings and independent supports should be eliminated. Far too much good has accrued from these changes to the service system. It does suggest however that leadership must be aware of the potential for increased risk when assigning staff and establishing methods for training personnel and providing supervision and technical assistance to staff. Dispersed supports may increase the probability of human error; therefore this increase in risk needs to be accounted for.

- **Technical programs.** Many person-specific programs and support plans are extremely complex and written in technical and "dense" language that results in staff interpretation errors (e.g., "winging it") that can differ from what the clinician expected. The more technical and complex a procedure, the greater the risk of human error. When possible, simplify protocols and use plain language to describe what staff needs to do.

- **Lack of training and supervision.** Very often there is a relative dearth of direct "hands-on" training, practice and supervisory oversight associated with support plans and complex procedures in I/DD settings. Personnel are expected to understand exactly how to perform tasks, even when they may be novel or complicated. Inadequate training and direct supervision can lead to substantial variation in how a procedure is actually implemented. This variation only serves to increase the probability of human error and the potential for an adverse event.

5. **DEPENDENCE ON PEOPLE.** The delivery of support and services to persons with I/DD is a very "labor intensive" business that is almost exclusively dependent upon people (staff and personal assistants) doing something for or with an individual. Unfortunately, people make mistakes! Activities and processes that are dependent upon people are therefore quite prone to human error. It is important to recognize this simple fact. Systems must be designed with an understanding that errors and mistakes <u>will</u> take place. Support systems and programs for individuals need to be designed to avoid reliance on *errorless* performance since that simply will rarely, if ever, be present in the "real world." Expect that mistakes will sometimes happen and build in methods to reduce the probability and/or the impact of those mistakes. [Note: the risk management procedure called Failure Mode Effects and Analysis is designed to do that. Interested readers may wish to explore this tool in greater detail.]

6. **INADEQUATE TIME.** When staff do not have enough time to properly complete tasks they often end up "rushing" and using shortcuts. This in turn can result in staff "unofficially" altering protocols and written procedures in order to "get it done" on time. When this happens the steps in complex tasks become more tightly coupled and completed more quickly without providing

time to address problems or errors that take place in the previous steps of a procedure. When staff are rushing they tend to feel overwhelmed and anxious. This associated stress can increase the probability of mistakes and errors.

It is not uncommon in many I/DD programs for far too many specific activities and tasks to be scheduled in a very compressed time period. This is particularly true within formal residential programs, especially during the morning and early evening. During these periods many competing tasks must be completed in a limited amount of time. All too often performance evaluations are based on whether or not staff complete required tasks in the allotted time, not on whether the tasks and activities are actually conducted in a safe fashion. Program managers should therefore carefully evaluate what they expect to be performed and whether or not the amount of allotted time is sufficient for required activities to be safely conducted. They should also think carefully about the unintended consequences of management expectations (e.g., quantity and timeliness versus safety of staff actions).

7. **DISTRACTION.** It is not unusual for residential, employment/day, recreation and even transportation services and program settings to be confusing environments that contain multiple visual distractions, are loud and noisy (many people talking at once), and have different individuals vying for attention all at the same time. Such distraction can easily serve to divert the attention of staff as they attempt to complete complex procedures or implement a highly technical program or task. This can lead to the potential for mistakes and errors that can result in an adverse event, sometimes one that causes injury or harm to an individual. A few examples of distractions could include any of the following:

- The phone rings when a staff member in a residence is preparing a special diet. She forgets exactly what to do next;

- Another individual interrupts and asks a question of a staff member when preparing medications for distribution and administration. He miss counts and fails to provide all the necessary medications;

- Two individuals become agitated and begin arguing with one another. This leads to a staff member temporarily leaving another person unattended whom they were assisting prepare a meal on the stove. This person burns their hand on the stove.

PEOPLE CHARACTERISTICS THAT CAN INCREASE ERROR. In addition to program and setting factors that can increase risk of human error, there are some special characteristics of the people who are supported in I/DD programs that can pose especially high risk and should therefore always be carefully reviewed to enhance safety and improve quality within your organization. Some of these more important "people" characteristics include:

1. **IMPULSIVE BEHAVIOR.** Individuals with impulsive behavior require especially vigilant supervision since they are often "driven" to engage in potentially harmful behaviors. Very brief periods of inattention can sometimes result in opportunities for the impulsive behavior to manifest itself. Some common examples of risk associated with impulsive behavior include:

    a. Impulsive food ingestion, including pica

    b. Self-injury

    c. Aggression towards other people

    d. Sexual offending

    e. Running away from required supervision (e.g., AWOL)

2. **INJURIES AND ILLNESS.** The presence of injuries and/or illness in persons with limited communication skills sometimes makes it very difficult to correctly identify and diagnose a potential problem that may require timely intervention. Consequently, injuries and serious illnesses can sometimes go unrecognized until they have progressed and result in observable signs or have become extremely painful or debilitating.

3. **LIMITED MOTOR CONTROL.** Individuals who have significant physical disabilities are at an increased risk of harm in activities that require motor control. Lifting and transfer, bathing, transportation, sleeping and other types of activities where the absence of an ability to stand, sit, roll over and exercise trunk control can pose special risks. A very special concern that should always be considered is the risk of falls in this group of people.

4. **MEDICATIONS.** Individuals with I/DD often receive relatively complex medication regimens that require very careful administration and close observation for harmful side effects. It is not unusual for some individuals to have a variety of different health care providers, each of whom prescribes medication, and sometimes without the timely awareness of the other medications a person is receiving. In addition, many individuals with I/DD receive potent psychotropic medications that can have relatively serious side effects if not adequately monitored. These situations, along with the prescription of drugs that must be maintained within a very narrow therapeutic range, place certain individuals with I/DD at heightened risk of harm.

5. **SPECIAL DIETS.** A number of persons who have very severe intellectual and physical disabilities receive special diets that can involve the need for specific and careful preparation of foods along with the implementation of highly individualized feeding protocols. The presence of a swallowing disorder makes this group of individuals extremely vulnerable to choking and aspiration.

6. **COMMUNICATION SKILLS.** Many of the people who receive support in I/DD programs may have limited communication skills, particularly the inability to use verbal communication. Some people have difficulty communicating to staff and others when they are experiencing distress, pain, anxiety, anger or

confusion. The absence of good verbal communication skills requires staff and others who provide support to be especially vigilant in picking up on and properly interpreting non-verbal signs. This requires knowledge of the person and careful attention to body language and overt behaviors that may be a sign that something is wrong and that immediate assistance is needed. Very often these non-verbal cues are unique to each person and require experience and familiarity with the individual to be properly interpreted.

7. **INDIVIDUALIZED SUPPORT PLANS.** Certainly one of the most important aspects of providing meaningful and effective support to people with developmental disabilities is the use of very personalized and highly individualized support plans. This greatly improves the quality and appropriateness of supports. However, with that benefit comes an increase in risk of error that simply must be recognized and addressed. As noted earlier, a common method in many other industries for increasing safety and reducing the probability of error is to focus on standardization of tasks and activities – in other words, a procedure is performed exactly the same way every time, by everyone. The use of individualized programs means that tasks and activities are not designed using a "cookie cutter" approach. Therefore, staff are required to remember many different ways of providing a similar service or support that is tailored to an individual service recipient and his or her unique needs and preferences. This difference in "how something is done" inevitably introduces a risk of error. This doesn't mean individualized service and support planning should be discontinued. That would be a travesty and negatively impact on the quality of life for persons with a disability. It simply means supervisors, program authors and managers in I/DD services organizations and systems need to be cognizant of this risk factor and continually put in place environmental cues, practical training and enhanced methods of supervision. They must also establish a true culture of safety and involve all stakeholders in the evaluation of the safety of services and supports on continual basis.

SPECIAL CONCERNS IN SELF DIRECTED SUPPORTS

MORE AND MORE I/DD service systems are embracing self-directed supports as a means of expanding choice and control by individuals and their families over what services they receive, who provides personal support and how that support is to be provided. This approach can greatly enrich the quality of life for individuals with disabilities. However, it can also bring with it a variety of unique risks that should be recognized and then addressed by the service system. In addition to the more common issues that can lead to adverse events and that are typically present within the more traditional service system, a variety of additional risks can sometimes present themselves for persons relying on self-directed supports.

Some of these additional risks that may be present in self-directed support and should therefore be taken into consideration include:

1. Hiring and retaining sufficient individuals to provide needed support;

2. Assuring proper background checks of support personnel;

3. Training of and developing critical skills for those who provide support;

4. Establishing backup systems to ensure support staff are available when scheduled and needed; and

5. Monitoring for and properly reviewing and investigating incidents of abuse and neglect

Systematic and easy to use methods for providing individuals with simple tools to help them manage the supports they receive are essential. It is equally important to make sure the individual and his/her circle of support and/or family has access to practical risk mitigation tools. Thus, the focus for those who design, manage and oversee I/DD services and supports needs to focus to a much greater extent on supporting the individual with the disability to safely manage their own supports.

ENHANCE QUALITY AND SAFETY BY MANAGING RISK EFFECTIVELY

ENHANCING SAFETY and promoting quality requires that all I/DD support organizations and service systems work hard to establish a robust and meaningful culture of safety. To do this they must continually work to develop and actively use analytic tools to identify problems and guide actions for preventing adverse events.

Some of these tools are presented in the books and on-line courses that are included in the **Risk Management in DD** series. As noted, the series is designed to help interested support personnel, managers, clinicians and other stakeholders apply practical approaches to risk mitigation and safety enhancement – tools that are tailored to the special issues and needs present in service programs and public and private systems that support people with intellectual and developmental disabilities.

Remember, analytic approaches to safety and quality and the use of techniques such as those presented throughout this series (e.g., root cause analysis, risk screening, mortality review, failure mode effects analysis, and incident management) – however, are just tools. They must be used properly by people who are skilled and trained. For these tools to be most effective, all the people within your organization must really believe that safety is important and that better quality in services is achievable. You can help them achieve this.

Bad things may happen to people with disabilities, but remember that you and your colleagues can make a big difference in reducing harmful events and increasing opportunities for individuals with a disability to experience a true quality of life. Continue your study by moving on to the next chapter; and then, to additional resources in the **Risk Management in DD** series.

CHAPTER 3

An Introduction to Root Cause Analysis in Developmental Disabilities

Root Cause Analysis in Developmental Disabilities has been designed for both experienced professionals and managers as well as for individuals who are just beginning their careers in organizations that serve persons with intellectual and developmental disabilities (I/DD) and who are interested in establishing structured approaches to the mitigation of risk for the people they support. The methods and materials outlined in the chapters that follow present a different way of looking at how to review and then prevent adverse events (unfortunate incidents that often cause harm to service recipients) from taking place in the future. The content in this book and its associated on-line educational course includes step-by-step directions and a variety of tools and printable forms and checklists for implementing the process of root cause analysis within an organization that supports people with I/DD.

WHAT IS ROOT CAUSE ANALYSIS? Root Cause Analysis (RCA) is a structured approach to the investigation, review and analysis of significant adverse events. In the fields of healthcare and human services it is designed to help organizations reduce the risk of harm for the people they serve and support. RCA is an analytic process that can help identify the underlying factors that have contributed to or have directly caused a serious adverse or sentinel event. The results of a RCA are utilized by organizations to guide and direct corrective changes to processes, the environment, and human behavior in order to prevent or reduce the probability that the adverse event will occur again in the future.

Adverse Events are undesirable incidents that cause harm or call into question the adequacy of care. Examples of adverse events in the field of I/DD include:

- a person who requires constant supervision is left alone and unattended in an employment program and goes missing for an hour and hurts himself when he falls down;

- an individual who requires a special diet chokes on food that was not properly prepared;

- the wrong dose of a prescription medication is administered by direct support staff in a group home.

Sentinel Events are more serious. They lead to death or substantial harm. They are adverse events that are unexpected and that place someone at significant risk of death or serious injury. Examples of sentinel events in the field of I/DD include:

- an individual drowns in the bathtub after being left temporarily alone;

- a person falls off a wheelchair lift and fractures his or her leg;

- an individual dies from asphyxiation while being physically restrained.

Almost every day, and all across the nation, errors and mistakes – and failures in the support system - lead to preventable injuries - and sometimes even death - for persons with intellectual and other developmental disabilities. National and local news frequently report on such events, temporarily highlighting "problems" and "abuses" that are present within the service system that serves people who are considered "vulnerable" and in need of special support. Pay attention to such incidents; they take place far too often and are unfortunately present even in the best service organizations and systems.

SOME BASIC PRINCIPLES OF RCA

ROOT CAUSE ANALYSIS is a tool for use following a significant adverse event in order to better understand what can be done to prevent a future occurrence of the same or similar type of event. It is a process of discovery that attempts to find out exactly:

- **WHAT** happened,

- **WHY** it happened, and

- **HOW** it can be prevented from happening again.

Consequently, the primary goal of RCA is *prevention*.

The proper use of RCA in the field of I/DD allows a service organization to focus on understanding the cause(s) of incidents, rather than blaming people when adverse events take place. It begins with the basic premise that errors and failures are usually the result of flaws in the system, not simply the action or inaction of people (such as direct support staff). Chapter 2 presented an overview of some of the more important principles of safety. Carefully review these. It is imperative that the leadership of I/DD service organizations understand these concepts and embrace them if RCA (or pretty much any risk mitigation tool) is to be effective.

Always remember that in order to accurately identify what has contributed to and caused an adverse event it is necessary to understand that:

- Adverse events are rarely the result of a single and isolated mistake. Rather, there is usually a "chain" of events that leads up to the adverse incident itself. Ineffective corrective action will only likely result if the focus is only on analyzing the proximate event (what takes place immediately before the adverse event). Take the time to identify and understand what led up to the proximate event.

- Error prone situations – not simply error prone people – usually lead to what we refer to as "accidents." Very often we will find faulty system designs at the beginning of the error chain that ultimately lead to the adverse event or "accident." That is why it is so important to look back at the entire chain of events to understand what may have set the stage for the human error to take place.

- People factors - such as momentary distraction, forgetting, misjudgment – are often the very last "link" in the chain of events that result in an adverse event. Since it is not practical to supervise every action taken by every staff member at every time, meaningful prevention should not attempt to focus simply on managing "human nature." Rather, effective prevention efforts need to focus on changing how the system is or is not facilitating safe and correct behavior and is avoiding systems faults that lead to or prompt human error.

- An emphasis on systems design and improvement is more effective than reliance on the individual discipline of employees. The assertive discipline of staff can appear to represent firm action that will prevent future adverse events. However, it tends to ignore the underlying reasons why staff may have made a mistake. A sole reliance on discipline therefore does little to actually reduce the probability that similar errors will take place with other employees. An organization that relies on discipline alone for correction of harmful incidents risks engaging in a "feel good" approach that may "look good" on a short term basis, but that will likely lead to the same type of adverse event repeating itself over and over again.

- Errorless performance by staff is a myth. The services and supports provided by staff in I/DD organizations are often complex and challenging. It is next to impossible to totally eliminate mistakes. But, it is possible to reduce their probability, and, their impact when they do occur. Since it is not possible to "program" people to be error-free, effective risk management strives to understand why errors take place and then to make changes to systems (i.e., training, protocols, equipment, staffing, etc.) in order to reduce the probability of the errors before they can result in another adverse event.

A meaningful approach to risk mitigation therefore requires a commitment to thinking differently about safety. This is what is meant by the concept "culture" of safety. Root cause analysis is one of many different tools that an organization can use to promote such a culture of safety. But, it is just a tool. For it to be effective, the people within the organization must believe that safety really is important. The organization must work hard to create the belief that how systems of support are designed can significantly impact the safety and quality of services.

INVESTIGATIONS v RCA

A ROOT CAUSE ANALYSIS IS NOT the same thing as an investigation, such as may occur following an allegation of abuse or other alleged wrongdoing. They are very different processes.

INVESTIGATIONS:

- Tend to focus on identifying exactly *what* happened and *who* was responsible
- The emphasis is on facts and findings that often result in assigning culpability
- In I/DD organizations staff disciplinary action very often follows from the findings of an investigation.

ROOT CAUSE ANALYSIS:

- The focus of RCA is on *why* something happened and *how* it can be prevented from happening again

- The emphasis is on *systems* factors that contributed to or caused the errors made by people – findings from the analysis are used to guide systems change

- RCA never looks to fix blame – discipline should never result from a properly conducted RCA

EXPLORATION OF CAUSE AND EFFECT. Root Cause Analysis involves a thorough exploration of cause and effect relationships. It requires a comprehensive review and analysis of human factors, organizational and support systems, and the formal and informal processes that guide the actions of people within the organization. It does this by directing a series of *why questions*, over and over again, to identify the actual and potential contribution different factors have had to causing the event under study. Once causative and contributory factors are identified, the process is repeated to uncover potential solutions and improvements to the system that can act as barriers and prevent future failures and thus similar adverse events.

IMPORTANT CONCEPTS AND TERMS

ROOT CAUSE ANALYSIS has been designed primarily as a risk management tool that can foster a greater understanding of why something "bad" has happened and what can be done in the future to prevent its reoccurrence. There are a few basic concepts and terms that are important to understanding and utilizing the process of RCA. These include:

1. **Adverse Event.** Any undesirable incident that causes harm or calls into question the adequacy of care.

2. **Barrier.** In root cause analysis a barrier represents a process, environmental change, or system that can prevent or reduce the probability of an adverse event.

3. **Brainstorming.** A process used with a group that encourages free thinking and leads to the generation of numerous ideas.

4. **Contributory Factor.** These are additional reasons, beyond the root cause, that an adverse event has occurred. They increase risk by setting the stage for or contributing to the probability of an adverse event.

5. **Incidental Finding.** Problems, inefficiencies or failures in a process or system that did not contribute to the incident under consideration but which require attention by the organization in order to prevent other types of adverse events.

6. **Proximate Cause.** This is the most obvious reason an adverse event occurred. Usually the proximate cause is identified in investigations. Often it reflects a superficial analysis, focusing on human error.

7. **Root Cause.** This is the most basic and fundamental or underlying cause of an adverse event. It is the "root" of the problem and must be addressed if prevention strategies are

to be effective. In most instances the root cause is a systems failure, not human error.

8. **Sentinel Event.** This is an adverse event that is unexpected and that leads directly to or places someone at risk of death or serious harm.

A BRIEF HISTORY OF ROOT CAUSE ANALYSIS

TO PROPERLY CONDUCT a good RCA it can be helpful to have a basic understanding of how it has evolved as a risk mitigation tool in other industries, as well as how the design of service systems and the presence of human error can influence and contribute to adverse events in the field of developmental disabilities. In order to more fully understand the critical role these factors play in causing adverse events, carefully review the information presented in Chapter 2. This information can help readers "think differently" about how to review and analyze adverse events and the many different incidents that are common to I/DD organizations and the process of delivering supports and services to people with disabilities.

As noted earlier, root cause analysis (RCA) is a structured and analytic process designed to help identify the underlying factors that have contributed to or have directly caused a major adverse event or systems failure. The results of the analysis are typically utilized to guide and direct changes to processes, the environment and human behavior in order to prevent or reduce the probability that the same adverse event will occur in the future.

Root cause analysis has been utilized in many different industries for the past three to four decades, originating in the field of engineering. It has expanded its reach to aerospace, transportation, nuclear power and chemical processing, pollution control, information technology and manufacturing.[1] More recently, RCA has become an important addition to the risk management armamentarium in the health care system, with the Joint Commission recognizing its potential and promoting the use of this technique for responding to sentinel events.[2] The movement to utilize RCA in health care was driven by a recognition that the health care system had become extremely complex and was experiencing an abnormally high rate of adverse events that were resulting in harm and even death to the consumers of the system. The results of such error in health care were (and are even today) quite staggering. According to the Harvard School of Public Health, it was estimated that in the late 1990's one million people were injured in the hospital, and between 44,000 and 120,000 people died each year as a result of medical errors. This was more than from motor vehicle accidents, breast cancer, and accidental falls combined.[3]

Given the extent of serious injuries and avoidable deaths resulting from preventable medical errors, the Institute of Medicine[4], as well as patient safety organizations across the U.S., concluded that patient safety could only be improved by increasing the focus on reducing faulty systems. Improvement to safety, it was determined, is best accomplished by embracing a systematic approach to *learning* from previous errors and mistakes and making changes to organizational processes – not blaming and punishing individuals. Root cause analysis became one of the preferred tools for doing such, and as previously mentioned, became a required risk management procedure in health care settings by the Joint Commission. More recently the benefits of RCA have started to become recognized by the home health care industry.

Therefore, if a structured risk management tool such as RCA is helpful in reducing errors in the healthcare field, can it be useful within the field of developmental disabilities? Most likely "yes" it can. After all, many of the very same factors that were and are present within acute and long-term health care, and that are directly related to increased error and harmful incidents, are also present within the field of developmental disabilities services. For instance:

1. We too serve hundreds of thousands of people with very different and very significant and specialized needs (severe cognitive and intellectual disabilities, complex medical conditions, physical disabilities, extremely challenging behavior, unique needs for close supervision, etc.).

2. We also have a service system that is growing and growing more complex every day (e.g., more and more diverse populations, ever expanding rules and regulations, service settings that are geographically distant and fully integrated, multiple service providers, increasing public expectation).

3. We too have a large number of adverse events, most of which we probably don't even know about (varied reporting requirements and methods, staff who work alone, historical organizational cultures that avoid use of data, overly laborious requirements for reporting that lead to avoidance, etc.).

Given these similarities, it can be reasonably expected that within the very near future the public, major funders such as the federal and state governments, and most importantly the persons receiving services and supports will demand the same level of scrutiny and attention to safety in the field of I/DD as has been required in health care. Although not yet widely reported in the field of I/DD, root cause analysis can and most likely will become an important tool for risk mitigation and quality improvement in the very near future.

OBSTACLES TO THE USE OF RCA

BY ITS VERY NATURE root cause analysis seeks to uncover and identify system "failures" and human errors that have contributed to something "bad" that has resulted in harm to a person. Uncovering failures and mistakes is sometimes antithetical to the mindset of managers and many legal advisors, who may instinctively try to mitigate or reduce exposure to criticism and damaging litigation. Unfortunately, such a traditional approach to adverse events serves to inhibit the development of a meaningful "culture of safety." It also does little to enhance a true understanding of the cause(s) of adverse events, prevent future incidents and promote safe practices and quality improvement in services. It is therefore important to recognize and address the very real potential for resistance to root cause analysis that may exist within a service organization.

When such resistance is present, an ongoing process of education, orientation and logical persuasion - throughout the organization, but especially within leadership ranks, should be implemented if RCA is to become an accepted tool for quality improvement and risk reduction. Therefore, it is very important to pay careful attention to the organization's "readiness" to accept and embrace analytic techniques such as RCA.

A Dynamic Dilemma. Many of the same issues now facing intellectual and developmental disabilities service systems have historically challenged the health care field in the recent past. This includes the inherent conflict so often associated with a need for critical and introspective review of how an organization's systems may actually increase the probability of human error versus the need to avoid blame, limit negative publicity and avert potential litigation. In industries such as transportation, nuclear power generation, engineering and aerospace, processes such as root cause analysis and related incident review procedures have been used for a long time as a means of identifying and correcting hazards. Managers and leaders in these fields are consequently aware of the benefits of careful and systematic analysis of actual and potential adverse events. However, in the field of intellectual and developmental disabilities the use of tools such as root cause analysis is relatively new. This lack of familiarity can contribute to resistance to the use of analytic methods that are designed to seek out and identify failures and problems within the service system. Public I/DD systems (e.g., state DD agencies) and private service providers tend to shy away from processes that can reveal and even highlight deficiencies in their management of services.

Organizational "readiness" is therefore imperative if root cause analysis is to be accepted and used as an effective safety enhancement and quality improvement tool in the field of intellectual and developmental disabilities. Quality managers and other leaders within an I/DD organization are encouraged to take the time to assess the readiness of their agency to embrace root cause analysis as an improvement tool before beginning to use it. This need for assessment is particularly true for legal personnel, senior managers and administrators. It is important to know whether or not an orientation designed to increase awareness of the benefits that can be achieved from instituting a more proactive approach to the prevention of serious adverse events is needed.

To assess the readiness of an I/DD organization a simple tool is provided in **Appendix B.** The completion of this checklist can help guide the development of a plan to overcome obstacles that may inhibit the effective use of RCA before starting to actually use it.

ERROR AND RISK

IN ORDER TO EFFECTIVELY USE RCA it is absolutely essential to have an appreciation for the role that human error can and so often does play in causing adverse events. Almost all adverse incidents that take place in the field of I/DD are the result of a chain of events that led up to an incident and the actions or failures to act that ultimately result in harm to an individual. Human error - mistakes, slips and deviations from practice - are almost always present within this chain. They very often represent the most important and critical contributory factors associated with the adverse event. Understanding why such error takes place is the goal of root cause analysis. Only by understanding why, can effective solutions be put in place that can prevent similar adverse incidents from occurring in the future.

The second chapter of this book goes into greater detail about the role of human error and its relationship to adverse events. Readers who have not carefully reviewed Chapter 2 are strongly encouraged to do so now. Without an appreciation for and true understanding of how human error influences risk it will not be possible to effectively use the technique of root cause analysis in a meaningful fashion.

A brief summary of some of the major concepts presented in the second chapter follows on the next few pages. However, cursory review of this material is not a substitute for a more thorough reading of Chapter 2.

Systems Set the Stage for Error. The systems within which professional and direct support staff work tend to be more responsible for adverse events then are the people themselves. As has been noted over and over again in the Risk Management in DD series, how the service system is set up and managed plays a critical role in causing many adverse events. In fact, the National Patient Safety Foundation[5] has established a basic philosophy that indicates the majority of errors in health care are caused by faulty systems that "set up" people to make errors that in turn result in adverse events. Therefore, it is not useful in the long run to simply hold staff responsible for mistakes; but, rather it is far more beneficial to work to identify how poorly designed processes can lead to errors in the first place.

There are a number of special factors that increase the risk of error and can result in adverse events in healthcare settings that have been identified for a number of years. To a very great extent, these same issues are present within the developmental disabilities service system and must be recognized so that inherent risks are mitigated where possible. These special risk factors can include:

- Variability
- Complexity
- Coupling
- Lack of standardization
- Dependence on People
- Inadequate time
- Other special factors in I/DD services

As noted, more detailed information on these special risk factors is presented in Chapter 2. A very brief summary of these issues and risk factors follows:

Variability. Variability increases risk of human error since it can lead to uncertainty over how to provide support to a specific person. In most disability service settings there are major differences in the needs and characteristics of the people being served and in the staff who serve them. Significant variability also can exist in the types of services and settings in which those services are provided (e.g., residential support, education, employment, transportation, medical and allied health). The individual nature of supports is a very positive aspect of I/DD services; but it carries with it an increased risk of error that needs to be recognized and addressed when planning for services and managing personnel.

Complexity. The complexity of the many different tasks and activities that direct support personnel must perform every day can contribute to error. When staff are asked to follow complex routines and implement highly specialized activities, the risk of error dramatically increases. Tasks such as feeding, medication administration, bathing, transfer for persons with physical limitations, and behavior management intervention – often in highly stressful situations -

are all high risk and complex processes that are prone to human error. When complex multistep processes must be precisely performed it is more likely that an error of some type will take place – and sometimes that error can result in a serious adverse event. This increase in the probability of error must be addressed when developing protocols, training and providing supervision, and support to direct line personnel.

Coupling. Coupling refers the extent to which the separate steps in a process follow each other in rapid succession. The less time there is between steps, the less likely it is that there is time to recognize and correct mistakes before the next action in the sequence is implemented. Tight coupling can lead to progressive errors; in other words, when an error occurs at one step in the activity, it may be impossible to perform the next step properly. Many of the tasks, activities and special programs used to support people with complex needs are tightly coupled, adding to the risk that an error will be made. Once again, this risk should be recognized and addressed when designing individual programs and intervention protocols.

Lack of Standardization. Many industries, such as aviation, medical care and manufacturing spend a great deal of time analyzing and developing protocols that standardize processes in order to reduce the probability that mistakes will be made. That level of standardization is often difficult in human services, where the concept of individualization is so important. As noted above, there is significant variability in the needs and characteristics of the people supported in I/DD service systems. Certainly, respecting diversity and individuality is paramount to assuring personal dignity and the personal quality of life for the individuals served and supported by service providers. However, it is important to recognize the role variability and the lack of standardized protocols can play in promoting mistakes. It is essential, therefore, to balance the need for individualized processes with safeguards that can better assure reasonable safety for tasks and activities that are prone to error and that can result in very serious incidents when such error takes place.

Dependence on People. Support to persons with I/DD relies upon people (family members, staff and personal assistants) doing something for and with an individual. But, remember that all people make mistakes; and activities and processes that are dependent upon people are especially prone to error. Service systems and individual support programs must therefore be designed with the recognition that errors and mistakes will almost always take place. They need to be designed to avoid reliance on "errorless" performance since it is simply not very practical to assume that staff will never make an error or mistake.

Inadequate Time. In many I/DD programs and settings there are often too many tasks that are scheduled in too short a period of time. Staff who support people with a disability may feel the need to rush an activity to fit in all that they need to accomplish in time for the next scheduled activity. In fact, staff are often judged on their ability to meet scheduled deadlines not on how well they perform a task. This can lead to makeshift changes in how a program is conducted, alterations in routines, tighter coupling within an activity, and just feeling overwhelmed and stressed-out. Each of these factors will increase the chance that an error will occur; and unfortunately, some of those errors may contribute to a serious adverse event.

Other Common Risks. As just reviewed, there are many situations that can increase the risk of harm in service settings serving persons with I/DD. Experience suggests that the following characteristics of people and programs can also contribute to a relatively high risk of adverse events:

- Impulsive behavior

- Injuries and Illness

- Limited Motor Control

- Medications

- Special Diets

- Communication limitations

Human Error. In order to really understand the context for adverse events and to develop the most effective strategies for reducing risk (goal of root cause analysis) it is necessary to recognize the role human error can play as a causative factor. An appreciation of the major types of errors and the omnipresent "error chain" will help make a root cause analyses more focused and effective.

As detailed in Chapter 2, two primary types of error should be considered whenever conducting a root cause analysis related to I/DD services:

- **Active Error:** These are errors committed by a person (usually direct support staff). They are typically associated with the proximate cause of the event. Active errors may involve a slip (unintended deviation from the procedure); mistake (poor judgment or reasoning, often associated with a new situation) or an unsafe practice (direct violations of rules or standards). Active errors are usually identified in investigations and they typically become the focus of disciplinary proceedings, plans for retraining and other remediative efforts.

- **Latent Faults:** These are errors in system design that can promote and contribute to active errors. These faults may not be immediately evident and are related to decisions and actions by management. They set the stage for later active errors by staff. Very often latent faults are not identified by investigations. Failure to address these systemic issues can lead to further incidents and adverse events.

Careful analysis of almost all serious adverse events will identify the presence of both active errors and latent faults. When conducting a root cause analysis look at the entire "chain" of events in order to identify the presence of latent faults in the system that may have contributed to active errors. Work backwards from the most obvious or proximate cause of an incident to identify any critical system design factors that may have set the stage for staff errors. Only then can truly effective strategies for prevention and improvement be established. This is what root cause analysis is all about.

CHAPTER 4
How to Conduct a Root Cause Analysis
Part I: Prepare

ROOT CAUSE ANALYSIS is a very structured process of discovery. It requires a small team to go through a series of specific activities to identify why something happened and how it can be prevented from happening in the future. RCA therefore requires time and effort. Because it is a structured and formal process, RCA can be relatively time-consuming and should not be used for every adverse event that takes place within an organization, lest it become too diluted and ineffective. It is therefore important for an organization to carefully establish guidelines on when to "pause" and take the time to use a more comprehensive approach such as RCA.

Be Careful of the Action Trap. Experience suggests that there is typically a "demand" for action following a serious incident, with a call to immediately "fix" the "problem." Such inevitable pressure to quickly respond can result in the selection of the most expedient process for "solving" the problem. Such a need for action can result in overly simplistic approaches to remediation and prevention that may superficially "manage symptoms" but fail to address the underlying causes of errors, mistakes and harmful incidents. Eventually, the same problem reappears. Some common signs of this type of *action trap* include:

- A rush to judgment, typified by statements such as *"The reason for this incident is obvious to me"*

- Blaming and finger pointing, such as *"It wouldn't have happened if that person had only ... "*

- A call for new rules without analyzing why something happened, such as when statements like the following are quickly made: *"What we need to do is require ... "*

- Recommendations for a quick fix such as *"All we need to do is re-train the staff and make sure everyone signs off ... "*

- Managers who immediately defer responsibility and say something like *"Just have the team re-review the program ... "*

Certainly immediate action is almost always required following an adverse event, especially when someone is seriously injured, suffers from abuse or when the incident results in an unexpected and potentially avoidable death. Such immediate action, however, should not be seen as the "final" solution; rather, it is usually best viewed as an intermediate step to collect facts (investigate) and implement temporary safeguards (protect). Such actions are necessary, but often are not sufficient conditions for assuring longer-term risk mitigation. Investigation and temporary protective actions are not incompatible with RCA and in fact represent essential <u>preliminary</u> activities in order to conduct a well-informed RCA. The review and analysis should go further however when a very serious incident occurs or there is a repetition of the same type of adverse event over time or across programs and settings.

CHOOSING WHEN TO USE RCA

WHEN DONE CORRECTLY root cause analysis is a demanding process. It takes time, requires preparation, relies on a team of 3 to 5 staff, and can result in findings and recommendations that challenge conventional "wisdom." It should not be used haphazardly and organizations should avoid the temptation to take shortcuts or eliminate steps in the process. Root cause analysis should be used when it is really needed; and, when it is really needed, organizations should invest the time and resources to do it correctly.

USE RCA when:

- The cause of a major system failure is not clear.
- There are multiple or repeated incidents that are ascribed to human error.
- There is a sentinel event that results in death or severe injury.
- There are a series of similar incidents that could have resulted in death or severe injury.
- There is sufficient time to gather information, complete an investigation, put together a team and "think" before making major changes to your policies, practices or service system.

DO NOT USE RCA:

- To review every single incident or system failure.
- When the reason is obvious.
- When there is not time to implement a formal and structured process of discovery.

As a general rule, organizations should be selective in the use of root cause analysis. They should try to maintain the integrity of the process and gradually build their capacity for rigorous introspection and the use of analytic problem solving.

HOW TO CONDUCT A ROOT CAUSE ANALYSIS

In most cases, a thorough RCA will need two to three team meetings (each lasting approximately 2-3 hours). Both before and after the team meetings, substantial work is required to properly prepare for the analysis and to clearly communicate the results and team recommendations. Applying the time and effort to perform a RCA properly will result in meaningful and useful findings that can effectively mitigate risk and prevent future adverse events that result in harm.

While many different scenarios exist for how to structure a RCA, the following 10-step process, divided into three distinct phases, will promote a successful review, analysis and improvement result.

10 Step RCA Process
for Use with I/DD Organizations

Prepare
Before Team Meetings

STEP 1 **Clarify** the Target Event	STEP 2 **Assign** the RCA Team
STEP 3 **Collect** the Information	STEP 4 **Organize** the Information

Analyze
The First Meeting

STEP 5 **Identify** Contributory Factors	STEP 6 **Group** the Factors

The 2nd -3rd Team Meeting

STEP 7 **Identify** the Root Cause	STEP 8 **Develop** Prevention Strategies

Report & Follow-up
After Meetings

STEP 9 **Write/Review** the RCA Report	STEP 10 **Collect** the Information

STEP 1: CLARIFY THE TARGET EVENT

IT IS EXTREMELY IMPORTANT that a RCA focus on a specific incident. The incident or event should be one that has or could have resulted in significant harm to an individual or group of individuals. Most often a very serious sentinel event that could benefit from RCA will be obvious, although sometimes (see Special Caution below) extreme care needs to be taken before agreeing to complete a RCA on a recent high profile incident.

Selection criteria: There are some special criteria that should be carefully considered when selecting an incident for a structured and in-depth review using RCA. Recommended criteria for review include the following:

1. The cause of the adverse event is not clear, i.e., it is not immediately obvious what may have resulted in the actions of staff that were associated with the incident.

2. The incident represents a true sentinel event that resulted in death or severe injury.

3. Human error was involved; e.g., staff acted contrary to clear and established procedures or policies or a mistake by staff contributed to the incident.

4. There have been other incidents similar to the one under consideration that have been associated with human error.

5. There have been a series of similar incidents that could potentially result in death or severe injury.

6. There is sufficient information and valid documentation available regarding the incident and preferably including a completed and thorough investigation.

7. The results of the RCA can and will be used to develop a quality improvement/risk reduction initiative and not disciplinary or punitive action.

Where to look. As noted previously, in many instances it will not be necessary to look very far to find a significant incident that requires careful review and that fits the criteria outlined above. In fact, it is not unusual for leadership to step forward and request a "special review" for very serious incidents.

In organizations that have established a culture of safety staff will usually help identify events that have led to or very easily could have resulted in harm to service recipients. Organizations that have a clear cut focus on safety will actively encourage and visibly reinforce staff who bring issues forward that could benefit from more focused review. However, not all organizations are necessarily at that stage of maturity with regard to safety and risk mitigation. Absent an active process of identification of issues for analysis by leadership and staff throughout your organization it is possible to identify candidate incidents using a variety of other sources of information commonly available in most I/DD organizations.

For example, as more and more state systems and provider agencies develop a capacity to record data, analyze and report on critical incidents and other service quality issues, a rich source of information is becoming readily available that can help identify safety and risk mitigation issues that could benefit from RCA. Potential sources of such data/information that may meet the selection criteria outlined above include:

- Abuse/neglect reports
- Unusual incident reports, especially those pertaining to severe injuries
- Mortality reports
- Restraint reports
- Medication error/occurrence reports

- Complaint reports, particularly those from service recipients/families that relate to health and safety concerns
- Agency management reports that include analysis of trends and patterns of events related to health and safety

Clarify the issue. Once an incident has been identified for RCA and before assigning team members, it is important to make sure the issue that is to be the primary focus of the review is clarified and clear to the RCA team leader and the agency management. This very essential step is sometimes overlooked only to present problems after the analysis has started. Such clarification is a leadership responsibility. Upper management, together with the individual who will lead the RCA team, must take time to clearly identify what specific incident is to be reviewed, why it has been selected, what the objectives are for the review, how the information will be used and who will receive what information regarding the RCA findings and recommendations.

At times leadership may want to combine a series of similar incidents for a single review. While it is possible to do this, it is not recommended. Combining incidents can lead to significant distraction, create a very lengthy review process, require a very large team and potentially confuse findings. A more fruitful approach is to conduct a series of more focused reviews, one for each identified incident and then to look for convergence of findings as a means of developing more broad-reaching prevention strategies.

SPECIAL CAUTION: Experience suggests that it is not uncommon for agency leadership to request a RCA for a recent event that has led to very negative publicity and/or that is either currently in or holds high potential for litigation. Very often these types of incidents are "high profile" and "politically charged." Sometimes they involve potential adverse action against a provider agency or hold the potential for sanctions against the state system itself. There is an immediacy of need for "action" by leadership in many such situations. In these types of situations extreme caution should be exercised before "jumping into" a RCA unless the system has had sufficient experience with formal analytic procedures such as RCA and is ready to use the results to promote quality improvement, not take adverse action against an individual or agency. In order for RCA to be truly effective it requires sufficient time to collect and analyze information, approach the review in an "unbiased" fashion that seeks to uncover system faults, and promote and enhance a "culture of safety." Forcing the process into an unrealistic and tight timeline can result in an incomplete and faulty analysis. Using the results to "punish" can (and most likely will) compromise the willingness of people to be "honest" and forthcoming about mistakes, errors and faulty system designs in the future. Therefore, frank and honest discussion of this issue should occur with your organization's leadership if they request a RCA on an incident such as that described above.

STEP 2: ASSIGN THE RCA TEAM

ROOT CAUSE ANALYSIS is a team process. It is dependent upon diversity of knowledge and opinion. It is best conducted using a small "interdisciplinary" cadre of individuals who can bring an unbiased and open mind to the review and analytic process and who have specialized knowledge and skills. Recognizing that the process will usually require a minimum of two meetings (typically about 3 hours each) and "homework" both before and in-between meetings, the ability of personnel to devote time to the review must also be taken into consideration.

Team membership: The development of an effective RCA team requires the right balance of knowledge, expertise and awareness of the incident under review. Since the RCA process also includes substantial preparatory work and efficient management of the team process, membership should also include at least one individual familiar with root cause analysis and an individual who has facilitation skills. In most instances a good mix of personnel for the team will include the following:

- A team leader who has knowledge about and experience with the process of RCA.

- A facilitator who can help manage the team meetings and keep participants focused on the issue at hand.

- One to two persons from the program unit, site or organization where the incident took place and who have knowledge about the individuals receiving support in the program/site, the staffing at the program/site when the incident occurred, agency policy and procedure, staff training and skills and, most importantly, the events that led up to the adverse event being studied.

- An individual familiar with any investigations and investigatory findings regarding the incident.

- An individual associated with quality assurance/improvement unit and with knowledge about regulatory requirements and the process of quality improvement.

- One to two persons with content expertise. Some examples of potential professional experts could include:

  - Medical issue - nurse, physician, PA
  - Behavioral issue - psychologist, behavior specialist
  - Feeding/choking - speech pathologist, nutritionist, OT
  - Medication issue - pharmacist, physician, nurse, PA
  - Supervision issue - residential or day program supervisor

Keep the team small. In most cases the team should include between 5 and 7 individuals. Larger teams will often become difficult to manage especially during the formal team meetings since most members will want to contribute information and opinion. Very often this can significantly increase the amount of time needed for the meetings and may increase the tendency for discussions to "wander" and take a different path from the major focus of the review. Discuss the need for establishing a "manageable" team with the administrative authority who will be responsible for sanctioning the team and appointing its members.

Provide the team with authority. It is extremely important that leadership within your organization formally establish the RCA team and officially appoint its members. The authorizing authority should set clear expectations throughout your organization regarding the importance of the RCA review and the need for full and complete cooperation with team member requests for time and information. This can be accomplished through direct communication with the leadership team or via a letter or memorandum appointing team members.

Roles and Responsibilities. Leadership within the team and each assigned team member should have clearly defined roles and responsibilities. Participating in a RCA team involves much more than simply attending meetings and sharing opinions. Each team member must contribute and prepare information before scheduled meetings. Recommended roles and assigned activities include the following:

- **Agency Leadership:** Select the incident for review, clarify objectives, communications, authorize the RCA team and formally appoint team members.

- **Team Leader:** Responsible for organizing and coordinating the RCA process. This includes a great deal of preparatory work associated with the collection of documents, organization of the information (e.g., sequence analysis), team orientation to the principles and process of root cause analysis, planning for team meetings (time, location, materials, agendas), leading the meetings, preparation of meeting minutes and draft reports and reviewing findings and recommendations with leadership once the RCA has been completed.

- **Team Facilitator:** Assists the team leader and help manage the team meetings. Specific activities can include distribution of materials before and during the team meetings, time keeping, re-direction of discussions to assure they remain focused and on track, chalk/white board notes during the meeting and, if possible, note-taking for use as an official record of meetings.

- **Program/Site Personnel:** These staff need to provide information regarding the program, site and organizational policies, procedures, staffing patterns, program content (and expectations), staff development and training, service recipient needs and supports and other information/documentation specific to the service/program where the incident took place. In addition, program team members should be prepared to provide detailed information regarding what preceded the incident, exactly what took place during the incident, and activities following the incident. Specific information and background regarding the personal support plan and specialized services and individual programs for the persons affected by the incident should also be readily available for team review.

- **Investigations Personnel:** This is the representative from the entity that conducted any formal investigation of the incident. He or she should be prepared to clarify findings and serve as a liaison for communicating any law enforcement or other external review/investigation of the incident.

- **Quality Management Personnel:** At least one staff member from the QA/QI unit in the organization should usually participate on the team. The assigned representative from the quality assurance/improvement unit should provide the team with information regarding regulatory requirements and historical reviews of the program/site where the incident took place. This team member should organize data regarding reportable incident patterns and trends, licensing/certification reviews (if applicable), special recognitions for the program, complaints, quality improvement initiatives by the program/organization where the incident took place and any other quality related documentation of relevance to the issue under review.

- **Content Experts:** Professional staff with specialized knowledge related to the type of incident under review need to be prepared to discuss best practice standards and protocols relevant to the issue(s) associated with the incident. They should provide, if requested by the team leader, relevant reference documents and resources. In addition to readily available materials, professional team members may want to conduct a literature review to make sure the most up-to-date information is available.

STEP 3: COLLECT INFORMATION

RCA IS AN ANALYTIC PROCESS. The "data" for the analysis is comprised of information gleaned from a wide variety of sources that can shed light on the incident under review, the environment within which it took place, the individual(s) affected by the incident and the organization and staff that were providing service and support at the time of the adverse event. Before the RCA team review begins it is critically important to identify what records, documentation and other information is needed to provide a thorough understanding of the target event. The RCA leader is usually responsible for securing this background information and for organizing it in a fashion that will expedite the team review. While each distinct incident will have unique records and documentation, in general the following are useful resources and should be collected following clarification of the target incident:

1. Investigation report(s)
2. Autopsy report (if applicable)
3. Police reports associated with the incident (if applicable)
4. Interviews (usually part of any investigation)
5. Service recipient file (including medical record and support plan)
6. Incident report(s) associated with the target incident
7. Other incident reports from the program/site where the adverse event took place to help establish any patterns or trends (6-12 mo. prior to and following the incident under review)
8. Staff notes/log for the time period immediately before and after the target incident
9. Photographs or physical materials involved in the incident
10. Pertinent policies, procedures, protocols, and guidelines of the organization where the

incident took place

11. Training records for staff working at the program/site where the incident took place

12. Staffing schedules for the program/site, including specific staffing at the time of the incident

13. Inspection or quality review records for the program/site and/or organization

14. Program/site description

15. Sequence analysis and associated flowchart(s) prepared by knowledgeable staff that summarize exactly what happened in chronological order.

STEP 4: ORGANIZE THE INFORMATION USING SEQUENCE ANALYSIS

ONCE ALL OF THE PERTINENT and available documents have been gathered and copied it is necessary to organize the information so that a clear and logical sequence of events can be developed. Very often this will entail substantial preparatory work and is best accomplished by one individual to avoid confusion and duplication of effort. Usually the team leader assumes this responsibility although it can be assigned to another team member if they are familiar with the process and have intimate knowledge of the target adverse event that is being reviewed.

Sequence Analysis. A sequence analysis provides the "raw data" for an RCA by objectively summarizing exactly what happened and in what order it happened. The desired outcome from this step is the completion of a thorough chronological listing of what took place prior to, during and immediately after the incident. In essence, a sequence analysis is simply a detailed log of events: "first this happened, then that happened, then this, and then this ... " The sequence analysis should focus on factual information only. By identifying what actually took place and in what order events occurred, a structured sequence analysis will help the team avoid "assumptions" and potentially biased "conclusions" about the incident. It will also provide necessary information for identifying what factors may have contributed to any errors that resulted in the adverse event.

Use a Sequence Analysis Form. It is not unusual for different documents to contain different "pieces of the puzzle" that must be integrated together to form a comprehensive "picture" that includes all of the information associated with and pertinent to the adverse event. The use of a simple sequence analysis form can help structure this activity. A useful format for a sequence analysis is basically a table that includes five (5) columns and multiple rows (one for each recorded event). The column headings will usually include:

1. Date
2. Time
3. Person (who was involved)
4. Event (brief summary description)
5. Reference document and reporter

Using a table from a word processing program can expedite the development of a sequence analysis since you are able to insert rows as new information is gleaned from your review of different documents. To develop a sequence analysis you first create a table and then take one document (e.g., investigation report, staff log, interview note) and write down the date, time (if available), the people involved and a description of what happened. You then write down a reference (using codes can be helpful). You move rows around so that the earliest event comes first, followed by the next event, using the time and date as the primary and secondary sort criteria. When you have finished with the first document you go the next document and repeat the process, adding rows as necessary so that all events (regardless of document source) are arranged in chronological order. This process is continued until you have added information from all of the documents that you have gathered. **Appendix C** contains a sample format for developing a simple sequence analysis and **Appendix D** contains an example of part of a completed sequence analysis to help demonstrate the process.

Cautions When Developing a Sequence Analysis. Inevitably a number of issues or problems will arise when developing a sequence analysis. Some of the more common problems, and a few recommended solutions, include:

- **Privacy Concerns.** To help safeguard privacy it is preferable to use abbreviations for staff and service recipient names. A reference document that lists the actual names of individuals cross referenced to your codes can be maintained by the RCA leader and attached later on to the final report.

- **Unknown Time.** If the exact time of an event is not documented (and this often occurs) it becomes necessary to estimate the time based on its position between prior and later events. Estimated times can be noted with a footnote or asterisk.

- **Contradictory Information.** Sometimes information from different documents conflict with one another. It is usually best to use the information from source documents such as interview notes rather than reports that summarize information if they are contradictory. However, it is not uncommon for multiple interviewees to provide different accounts of an event. When this happens show all of the information (noting possible differences and contradictions in observations and reporting).

- **Length of Time for Inclusion.** Very often investigation reports will include substantial information pertaining to events or activities that took place well before the incident under review. This is done to provide perspective. Common examples include information related to staff training or discipline, other similar adverse events, support planning and program development, medical exams, diagnoses and prescriptions and other potentially pertinent information. If this information appears to be important for gaining a comprehensive understanding of factors that may have influenced or contributed to the adverse event that is under review, include it in your sequence analysis. If it does not appear factual and/or is unrelated to the event, you can leave it out of the sequence analysis but note that it is available and where it can be found. But, remember, it will be important for the RCA team to understand potential latent faults in the system that may contribute to the more immediate and proximate causes of an adverse event. When in doubt, provide the background information.

STEP 5: ILLUSTRATE THE SEQUENCE WITH A FLOWCHART

IT IS OFTEN HELPFUL to flowchart the main events from your sequence analysis. By using a flowchart you can visually illustrate what happened before, during and after the adverse event. Such visualization can provide a quick picture of important events, make it easier to identify potential linkages and, equally important, allow you to see any inconsistencies or mistakes in the sequence before you bring it to the team. Flowcharts are an excellent analytic tool for a number of other reasons:

- Flowcharts illustrate flawed processes. If you can't easily show a process, it's not functional and should be revised. Use of flowcharts for illustrating existing or planned procedures is therefore an excellent diagnostic and quality improvement tool.

- Flowcharts help visualize what happened - or what should happen and therefore allow you to compare an actual event sequence with a procedural requirement.

- They can help locate critical points to insert "barriers" or actions that might prevent an error from taking place in the future. Many word processing and presentation programs include flowcharting symbols and tools that are relatively easy to use.

Special Note: Throughout the process of root cause analysis there will be numerous instances where participants will be tempted to issue value statements or pass judgment on the actions of others. Common examples include phrases such as "That's terrible," "What were they thinking," "How stupid can you get," "Doesn't anybody care," "What a mess," etc. All team members must be reminded that hindsight is often crystal clear and that it is easy to look back and find "fault." Placing blame may "feel good," but it does NOT lead to constructive solutions. RCA must focus on the facts to be effective. Therefore, it important for the team leader, both in developing the sequence analysis and during team meetings, to actively stop such thinking and verbalization. If not, bias and opinion may adversely impact the analysis and findings, leading to faulty and potentially incorrect "solutions." Also, equally important, the process will become viewed as potentially punitive, seriously compromising efforts to establish an open and positive culture of safety.

SCHEDULE 1ST MEETING

THE FIRST RCA TEAM MEETING can be held once the first four steps (selected and clarified the specific adverse event for review, assigned the team, collected background information and documentation and organized the information into an integrated sequence analysis) have been completed. Formal communication to all team members (with a copy to the administrative leader who appointed the team) should include the date, time and location of the first meeting and a summary of background information re: the case that will be reviewed. A copy of the sequence analysis and flowchart can be sent prior to the meeting so members can familiarize themselves the event they will be analyzing. All team members should be reminded of the importance of privacy and confidentiality until the final report is issued and permission is granted by leadership for sharing information.

CHAPTER 5
How to Conduct a Root Cause Analysis
Part II: Analyze

ONCE ALL OF THE BACKGROUND work has been completed, including the development of a sequence analysis and associated flowcharts it is time for the first RCA team meeting. This meeting will usually take 2-4 hours, depending upon the complexity of the case and the experience of team members with the RCA process. Careful preparation prior to the meeting is essential. Make sure a time and place has been selected that is both convenient for team members and conducive to private discussion and uninterrupted analysis.

The following factors should be considered when setting up a RCA meeting:

1. **Meeting location.** Select a location that is centrally located to minimize any one team member having to travel unreasonable distances. Although this is sometimes not entirely possible, consideration for the time and effort involved in participating in the RCA by all team members is important and will send the right message.

2. **Materials.** Assemble all needed materials, including copies of handouts and pertinent documents prior to the first meeting. A flip-chart or large whiteboard, with markers will be necessary, along with a computer and projector, when available. These tools can be used when illustrating any flowcharts or other documentary materials. Copies of the sequence analysis, a brief summary statement of the adverse event under review, the RCA Report Form, a Summary of RCA and other important resource documents (e.g., investigation reports) should be available for use by team members. See **Appendix E** (Checklist for Team Leaders) for a listing of basic materials that will be needed for the first meeting.

3. **Meeting room.** Select a room that will be large enough for all team members to sit comfortably and one that is relatively "quiet" and private. Make sure there is a conference table that will permit members to lay out papers and materials and have direct face-to-face contact. Since the RCA process will usually require the use of flip-charts or other large writing surfaces (e.g., whiteboards) make sure there is ample wall space for display.

4. **Outside communication.** To the extent possible all team members should focus on the meeting and not be interrupted by outside telephone calls or other interruptions.

5. **Meeting rules.** Review with team members some general Meeting Rules and Principles to make sure everyone appreciates the need for a formal and structured approach to RCA. This will also make it easier to "correct" meeting participants when and if they deviate from good RCA practices. **Appendix F** has a simple listing of useful meeting rules that can serve as a reference guide and even be handed out to meeting

participants as a gentle reminder of expected meeting behavior.

6. **Orientation.** Remember that everyone may not be familiar with RCA and the purpose and outcomes that are expected. Therefore, provide members with a written Summary of RCA and briefly review the RCA Report Form so all members will understand what is expected and what the desired outcomes of the process are.

7. **Schedule.** The completion of the RCA will usually require between two and three meetings of the team. Each meeting will generally take between 2 and 3 hours, although the final meeting may be shorter if general consensus has been reached on the primary causes of the adverse event and recommended strategies for risk mitigation.

STEP 6: IDENTIFY CONTRIBUTORY FACTORS

THE IDENTIFICATION of the more important factors that contributed to - set the stage for - the adverse event under review is the "heart" of root cause analysis and should occur during the first team meeting. Remember, the purpose of the entire RCA process is to unveil why the incident took place, with a primary focus on what variables may have allowed errors to occur that ultimately resulted in something "bad" happening. The purpose is not to identify who made a mistake but rather why the error occurred. It is important for the team leader to repeatedly remind team members of this central principle since there may be a strong tendency to "fall back" to traditional ways of reviewing incidents that focus on finding fault and determining who to blame.

Review the Target Incident. Once the initial orientation has been completed it is time to review the incident and identify the proximate cause. The team leader or other designated individual should first provide background information about the individual and setting in which the incident occurred. Basic information regarding the individual that should be briefly presented includes age, gender, type and level of disability, medical and health-related concerns, behavioral issues (if any), history (keep it brief), prior similar incidents and the living and working situation at the time of the incident. If the incident took place within a residential setting, a brief description of the program or type of residential support should be provided. If it took place within a work/day program setting, a brief description should also be provided. The purpose of the background information is to provide a context for understanding what took place and what factors may have been important in causing the adverse event.

Next, describe in objective and factual terms what happened and what the most likely proximate cause was. The proximate cause is the event, activity or omission that immediately preceded the adverse event. [For example, if an individual chokes on a piece of food, the proximate cause would be providing the person with the food item.] Very often the assumed proximate cause will be clear from an investigation report. It is not unusual for the proximate cause to reflect some form of human error (e.g., someone did something they weren't supposed to do or didn't do something they were supposed to do).

At this point team members should seek clarification for any confusing or contradictory information related to the incident itself. The note taker/facilitator should document any new information.

Review the Sequence Analysis. Next, the team should review the sequence analysis (it should have been prepared ahead of time) and request that any team members who were directly involved in or have specific knowledge of the case describe exactly what happened in their own words. If a flowchart was prepared that reflects the major components of the sequence analysis it should also be reviewed. It can be helpful to visually project the flowchart and "walk-through" each step to help assure everyone fully understands what transpired before, during and immediately after the incident.

> The team leader and/or facilitator should make sure he/she allows for questions and modification of the sequence based on team member input. It is not unusual for the sequence analysis and accompanying flowchart to require modification once all team members have had an opportunity to review it and provide new information. The team leader, or other designated individual, should make hand-written corrections on a master document and inform the team that a revised and formal document will be provided at the next meeting or via email prior to the next meeting. Do not try to retype the sequence analysis during the meeting itself as this can become distracting and consume a great deal of time.

Compare to Written Procedures or Standards. Following any revisions to the sequence analysis, have team members compare what actually transpired to what would have been expected to take place. This can be accomplished in a number of ways. If there is a specific requirement, written procedure, individual program, guideline or other document that establishes process standards, list the steps or flowchart the process. Then compare what happened to the required process and identify major differences.

If there is no established procedure or program, the content expert on the team should then describe what best practice standards would require and contrast that with what actually happened. Look for differences: *"This should have happened, but instead this did."*

This process of comparison will help to highlight deviations and errors that took place before, during and after the adverse event. Identifying these critical error points will allow the team to focus the analysis on latent faults and active errors; this in turn will facilitate efforts to understand why those errors may have taken place (i.e., what were the contributory factors).

Remember that most errors stem from a "chain of events" and therefore it is important to "look" far enough back to capture all important causes, including systems faults. If the focus is only on the most immediate errors or faults the analysis will probably omit valuable information that could be used to design truly effective prevention strategies in later stages of the process.

CONTRIBUTORY FACTORS AND ERROR

WHEN BEGINNING TO IDENTIFY the errors that appear to have taken place in the chain of events leading up to the adverse event, the team should then start to examine exactly what type of error occurred and what factors may have contributed to or caused the error(s). This is the "meat" of root cause analysis. It is not sufficient to know that mistakes occurred - you need to identify WHY those errors took place. The reasons "why" represent the contributory factors and will guide the development of meaningful prevention efforts. To complete this critical stage of RCA you need to:

1. Understand the types of error that occurred

2. Identify multiple causes or contributory factors that influenced the errors

3. Classify those contributory factors so you can group them later on

Understanding Human Error. It is extremely important to think carefully about and understand the *type of error* that is identified in the causal chain of events. As the team reviews each of the critical error points from the sequence analysis it should classify the type of error that took place (see the second chapter for more detail). It is not necessary to formally document this classification, but the team should use the categorization as a mental prompt for exploring the most probable contributory factors.

Active errors are those typically committed by front-line direct support staff and usually take place close to the adverse event. There are three basic types of active errors that should be considered:

1. **Slips** or unintended deviations from intended or prescribed practice - the person does not do what they intended to and should have done. While there can be many different reasons for slips, some of the more common ones involve insufficient knowledge or skill, distraction, inattention and forgetfulness.

2. **Mistakes** are errors that occur due to faulty reasoning - the person does what was intended but it is the wrong thing to do. Very often these types of errors are associated with planning activities or take place when an individual is in a novel and unique situation that requires a new type of response and on the spot decisions.

3. **Unsafe Practices** take place when an individual consciously and deliberately engages in a high risk behavior or makes a decision to violate a known rule or standard. These types of errors tend to be infrequent and are not typically driven by malevolent motives.

Latent faults, on the other hand, represent systems-based errors and set the stage for slips, mistakes and unsafe practices by line personnel. Latent faults are often distant from the adverse event itself., and are therefore often overlooked. However, if they are not properly addressed latent faults will continue to "silently" operate and establish the context for future active errors. Pay special attention to the identification of latent faults as potential contributory factors.

Why Classify and Examine Errors? Understanding the type of error that took place will facilitate identifying appropriate contributory factors - the potential causes for the error. This is critical for the design of meaningful and properly targeted prevention strategies; in other words, in order to prevent future errors you must understand why past errors happened. Simply identifying that an error took place is not sufficient and will not lead to effective risk mitigation.

CATEGORIES OF CONTRIBUTORY FACTORS

There are a multitude of different contributory factors or potential causes for errors. Most can be grouped into common categories. **Appendix G** (Common Factors Checklist) provides a tool that can be used by RCA teams for grouping identified contributory factors to guide the review process. This checklist includes a number of common factors that can influence error in I/DD programs. The checklist can be a helpful tool for quickly reviewing each major category. Team members can use it to check off factors they believe may have caused each of the identified errors as they proceed in the analysis. Some of the more important factors listed on the checklist include the following:

Staff factors: Include personnel related issues that can lead to human error, such as:

- Required workload was not consistent with task demands or available staffing
- Staff skills and knowledge were not adequate for the type of tasks that had to be performed in a safe and competent fashion
- Experience with the service recipients or the tasks was not adequate
- Task priorities were not properly established or were wrong, such that critical tasks were not performed in a timely fashion
- Insufficient time was allocated for the required tasks (i.e., staff had to "rush," making slips or mistakes more likely)
- Teamwork and collaboration between personnel and others were inadequate or absent
- Poor relationships existed between staff resulting in performance problems
- Relationships with service recipients were problematic

Service Recipient factors: Include issues and risk factors related to the person(s) receiving support that can contribute to the error and/or the adverse event, such as:

- The individual exhibited poor adherence to prescribed activities related to self-care and safety – including the absence of appropriate supports or prompts for signaling safe actions
- Service recipient skills and knowledge were not sufficiently present for the performance of tasks in a safe and competent fashion
- Person(s) receiving support were in a novel situation with new and unique task demands
- The individual did not have the necessary physical or cognitive ability to perform the task in a safe fashion
- The individual was not able to communicate effectively with support personnel or others
- The individual's medical and/or behavioral status deteriorated very quickly or was extremely complex and required very specialized intervention
- The individual had problematic relationships with others

Assessment and Planning factors: Include incomplete and/or inadequate assessment, diagnosis and support planning that can increase error in the delivery of supports and services and lead to an adverse event. A few factors in this category include issues such as:

- Clinicians and support personnel did not provide a complete or accurate behavioral assessment and/or behavioral intervention
- Clinicians and support personnel failed to provide accurate and timely medical evaluation, diagnosis and/or health related services
- A proper assessment of physical risk was not carried out in a timely fashion
- A timely and complete process for support planning was not conducted or did not adequately address important support needs. Risk screening or evaluation was not conducted or did not identify critical risks

Other categories that should be carefully considered – and that are listed on the Common Factors Checklist include:

- Individual consumer factors
- Information and communication
- Assessment and planning
- Equipment and supplies
- Environment
- Organizational and leadership factors

Remember that each mistake, deviation and slip – in other words, each error - will most likely have a different configuration of factors that set the stage for the mistake/deviation/slip to take place. Some will be obvious, some not so.

When the team has finished reviewing the checklist, ask the members to brainstorm additional factors or variables that were not yet identified. **Appendix H** (Brainstorming Principles) presents a simple summary of the brainstorming process that can be used as a handout. It is important for all team members keep an open mind. The team meeting facilitator should actively encourage everyone to "throw out" different ideas. The use of a whiteboard or flip-chart to record new factors identified by the team can be very helpful in this regard. Once it seems as though the meeting participants have exhausted possibilities have the team go back and then evaluate each new idea.

Caution: During this stage of the process it is not unusual for the discussion to deviate to other issues and different types of adverse events. Remind the team to stay focused on the specific incident they are reviewing. Careful facilitation of the team process is critical during this stage to balance the need for freedom to share creative ideas with maintaining focus on the task at hand.

DRILL DOWN

FOR EACH MAJOR CONTRIBUTORY FACTOR that is identified the team must ask "why?" When doing so it is necessary for the team to keep going further back in the contributory chain by "drilling down" to the next level of causation. For example, if the review suggests that there was a slip and that a staff member was not aware of the need to turn off the electric switch on a wheelchair when on the lift, the team must ask "Why was he/she not aware?" If the answer to that question is "He/she forgot the procedure that was provided during training 18 months ago," ask "Why did he/she forget?" Keep drilling down by repeatedly asking "why." In this example, the team might find that the reason the staff member forgot the procedure was because (a) the training did not include any hands-on practice, or (b) the training was included along with other complex material many months ago, or (c) the staff member was never observed operating the lift and feedback was never provided, or (d) there was no posting in the van of the critical steps to the procedure (e.g., "Make sure you always ... "), or (e) the staff member was rarely called upon to transport individuals using the wheelchair van and it was a novel situation. For each of these reasons, continue to ask "why."

Of course an alternative scenario for the same example might be that the involved staff member was aware of the need to turn off the switch but elected not to (unsafe practice). In this instance, when the team asks "why," it might discover that the reason for making such a decision to not turn off the switch was because (a) the wheelchair switch was malfunctioning and wouldn't always turn back on, or (b) he/she was late for the pick-up and needed to move people quickly, or (c) he/she had never seen or personally experienced any accidents when the switch was left on, etc.

The discovery of the right "why" is absolutely critical for identifying the correct root cause and selecting the most appropriate and effective prevention strategies. Spending sufficient time on this phase of a RCA will be well rewarded later on in the process.

In many instances there will be multiple reasons or contributory factors that are identified by the team. They should all be noted; then the team can later on pick out those that appear to be the most fundamental (least common denominator). These will eventually become the focus of the analysis. This process should be repeated for each of the critical errors that are identified before proceeding to the next step in the RCA: grouping the contributory factors into clusters.

Appendix I (7 Common Reasons for Staff Error) contains a summary of possible reasons errors can occur in I/DD programs and service settings. This summary can be a guide to help prompt ideas during this phase of the analysis. The listing can be copied and distributed to team members during the first meeting.

STEP 6: GROUP THE FACTORS

THE USE OF AN AFFINITY DIAGRAM (see **Appendix J** for an example) can facilitate the actual grouping of ideas and factors, and do so in a fashion that provides each team member an opportunity to participate in an equal fashion. There are many different ways to conduct this type of group process. One simple method that reduces the potential bias and influence of one or two more "dominant" team members involves the following steps:

1. The meeting facilitator writes on "post-it" notes the causes and contributory factors that have been identified to date by the team (use shorthand to limit the amount of writing).

2. Have team members get up and move the notes around on a whiteboard, grouping them into clusters that each member believes is most appropriate. [Usually the notes will be moved a number of different times by different team members. During this phase of the exercise each team member is free to move the notes from where another team member placed them.]

3. Have the team then discuss the groupings, making changes that reflect general consensus.

4. Reference the Common Factors Checklist (see **Appendix G**) and write down titles or headings for each of the groups or clusters.

5. Optional: based on discussion the team leader can draw lines between causes and factors that may influence or be related to other groupings.

6. Use the result of this exercise to help shape the Contributory Factors Diagram which will be developed next

As the team is grouping the factors they should continue to think of other reasons why the errors may have taken place. This is the point at which the team leader/meeting facilitator should be relentless in pushing the team to ask *"Why did the incident take place and why did the human error occur?"* and *"How did each of these factors contribute to the adverse event?"* Once the team has exhausted all possibilities, the meeting facilitator should reorganize the clusters. Then begin to prioritize the identified factors, rank ordering them according to importance with the most important on top to least important on the bottom of the listing or diagram. A wall chart or the whiteboard with post-it notes can be used to provide a visual representation of the information. The meeting facilitator should try to seek consensus regarding the priorities.

DEVELOP CONTRIBUTORY FACTORS DIAGRAM

The Contributory Factors Diagram is a standard method for illustrating the relationship between variables that have been determined to cause or contribute to errors and the resultant adverse event. It can be used after completing the Affinity Diagram. Although an optional step, this tool can provide the team with a powerful visual illustration of the inter-relationships between the adverse event or system failure, the proximate cause, and the identified contributory factors that led to the target problem. Through the use of such a visual representation, the team can often more clearly recognize the root cause as well as begin the process of identifying potential solutions related to each of the contributory factors.

The development of a Contributory Factors Diagram can be accomplished in a number of different ways. Index cards or post-it notes can be used and placed on a whiteboard or wall chart, or the identified factors can be projected on a screen using a computer program (e.g., PowerPoint) or transparencies and an overhead projector. Whatever the specific method, the goal is to visually depict all of the major variables related to the issue under consideration so that the entire team can better understand how the variables relate to one another.

> **Note:** The preparation of a Contributory Factors Diagram is not required in order to complete a RCA, although visual illustration of interrelationships are helpful to the team and those who will be using the results of the analysis. RCA teams can also substitute a Cause and Effect or Fish Bone diagram for the Contributory Factors Diagram if they are more familiar with that technique, or leave out any diagrams and simply note in the report the relationship between errors/failures and identified contributory factors.

When illustrating the diagram and relationships of the variables, the team should ty to establish a hierarchy, with the system failure at the top, followed by the proximate cause, followed by the categories of contributory factors - rank-ordered. **Appendix K** provides an illustration of the hierarchal arrangement typical for a Contributory Factors Diagram.

Each of the 1st level factors may contain multiple variables, resulting from the process of "drilling down" that the team engaged in earlier. These 2nd level factors are often the most important to identify since they can lead directly to focused solutions. They (2nd level) do not have to be visually illustrated on the diagram, but should be noted within the report along with a description the causal relationship. It can be useful to circle those factors that appear to be the most basic and fundamental cause of the incident, *i.e.,* those that, if corrected, would have the highest probability of preventing a future incident.

Adverse events with multiple causes can result in complex diagrams that are difficult to read and interpret. Since the purpose of a Contributory Factors Diagram is to facilitate understanding and show the interrelationships between variables, it is often more useful to limit the amount of information placed into any one diagram. To do this, it may be necessary to create more than one diagram. The first can be used to only illustrate the event, failure, proximate cause and major cluster headings. Follow-up diagrams can be prepared for each of the cluster groupings separately. The number of error and factors that are identified by the team will dictate the number and complexity of diagrams that are used..

THE SECOND TEAM MEETING

THE SECOND TEAM MEETING will typically take place a few days following the first meeting. In order to maintain continuity of thought a long delay between meetings (e.g., two weeks or more) is not advisable. Whenever possible, team leaders should attempt to schedule meetings relatively close together.

During the second meeting the team leader or meeting facilitator will review the sequence analysis and any modifications that have been made based on input during the first meeting. The team leader will then review the contributory factors that had been identified in the first meeting and ask for additional ideas or considerations. New information should be added to the whiteboard or flipchart.

If the team did not begin to group the factors during the first meeting this activity should take place during the second meeting. Following initial grouping of factors into like clusters, a preliminary contributory factors diagram should be developed and either projected or illustrated on a whiteboard/flipchart. Once consensus has been achieved, the team leader should "walk through" the RCA Report Form with team members to complete relevant sections.

Depending upon the amount of remaining time, the team can begin the process of identifying potential solutions during the second meeting.

Before ending the second meeting the team leader should make homework assignments with an emphasis on bringing back additional ideas on approaches to preventing the major identified errors and reducing the risks associated with the primary contributory factors the team has identified.

The date, time and place for the third and final meeting - if necessary - should be clarified before ending the second meeting. In addition, the team leader should briefly discuss the agenda and major tasks that will be completed in the next meeting.

In some instances a third meeting may not be required if the team has agreed upon prevention strategies, prioritized those strategies and agreed upon what recommendations should be included in the final report. Rather than hold a third meeting the team can agree to review the completed RCA Report Form and/or draft written report through the use of email or other means of communication. It is the responsibility of the team leader to coordinate this review process.

STEP 7: IDENTIFY THE ROOT CAUSE

ONCE ALL OF THE POTENTIAL contributory factors have been identified and organized, the team should zero-in on the most essential or root cause of the error/failure. The root cause is the most fundamental reason that led to the failure and that if corrected, would significantly reduce the probability that same type of failure would occur in the future. The root cause is the underlying cause of the errors that took place. It represents the "least common denominator" when looking at all of the primary contributory factors that the team has identified.

Many different factors can underlie the root cause. For example, sometimes the root cause can be related to problems with a prescribed process, e.g., when policy requirements are not consistent with best practice standards. In other instances, the root cause may be related to insufficient communication to or between staff. The root cause can be related to insufficient staff skills or knowledge. Other times it relates back to an organizational culture that stresses efficiency over safety.

It is usually necessary to combine one or two of the identified contributory factors to capture the essence of what the most important cause of the error/failure was. Fix the root cause and you reduce the probability that the same types of errors and failures will take place. If those errors or failures do not take place the risk of a similar adverse event is significantly reduced.

At times more than one root cause may be present, particularly in cases where multiple and somewhat isolated categories of contributory factors were operating to cause the adverse event. Consequently it is not possible sometimes to clearly identify a root cause. In such instances the team should move on and focus on solutions that address the 1st level contributory factors.

Illustration of an Identified Root Cause in Relation to
Contributory Factors

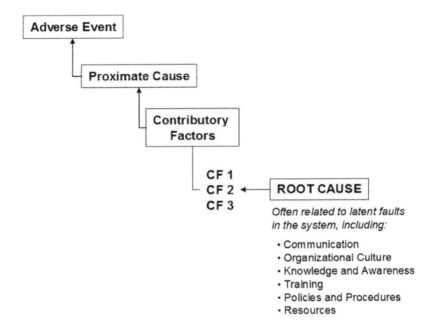

Remember, the whole purpose of a RCA is to identify what caused errors and failures that in turn were the cause of something bad happening. The root cause should therefore never be focused on an act of omission or commission by a person - but rather what was present or absent that allowed or set the stage for the omission or commission -or equipment failure - to have taken place.

STEP 8: IDENTIFY PREVENTION STRATEGIES

WHEN THE TEAM has reached consensus on what factors represent the most important causes of the error(s) that led up to the adverse event it is time to begin identifying solutions. Greater specificity in the analysis regarding causes will result in increased focus when identifying prevention strategies. That is why it is so important to drill down when analyzing contributory factors. Once the team really understands why an error was made, solutions will often become "obvious" and more easily generated.

Brainstorm Solutions. The solution phase begins with the meeting facilitator asking team members to brainstorm potential solutions that could address each cause and help prevent the same type of error from taking place in the future. This is done for each major grouping of contributory factors. The team should think about why someone did or didn't do something and what might need to be changed or adapted to prevent a slip, mistake, unsafe practice or other type of error. Members should discuss potential barriers that could automatically or physically interfere with or obstruct the error from taking place. [Remember, in RCA a barrier is any physical entity or procedure that blocks or reduces the likelihood of an action.] The team members should come up with multiple solutions and barriers for each of the factors/causes that were identified in the previous step. The Brainstorming Principles (see **Appendix H**) can be referenced by the meeting facilitator who should remind meeting participants to avoid evaluating or criticizing any of the suggestions that are offered at this point in the process. A designated member of the team (e.g., facilitator or note taker) can write down proposed solutions on large post-it notes that can be arranged along with the target cause on a whiteboard in the meeting room.

> **Note:** the completion of this activity may - depending upon time - represent a good point to end the second meeting. Before doing so the team leader should make "homework" assignments and ask members to think about more possible solutions before the third meeting. It is not unusual for creative ideas to come to light in between meetings when there is less immediate pressure to generate information and ideas in a short time period. Team members should also be reminded to seek information regarding potential solutions from a variety of different sources.

SEEK INFORMATION FROM OUTSIDE

MANY OF THE ISSUES your team will review are not unique to their organization. In other words, the same type(s) of adverse events, similar types of error and causes for those errors and failures have most likely arisen in other organizations, service systems and even other industries. Reviewing external resources can therefore be extremely helpful in generating solutions and ideas regarding effective preventive strategies. Effective risk management requires learning, often from the experiences of others. There are a few basic approaches to learning from others that can be utilized to enhance a RCA. These include:

Other Industries. It can be helpful at times to review the literature and conduct a search on the internet using key words that reflect the type of incident being analyzed. There are a number of very useful websites that can be accessed that may contain helpful information, including case studies. Many of these address issues more related to acute health care and hospital-based services; but it is possible to extrapolate from this literature by adapting the "problem" and "solution" to the particular situation present in an I/DD organization. For example, there is a wealth of information related to "falls" in the hospital and nursing home literature that is quite relevant to services for persons with disabilities. While there may be some differences in the specific populations served, the type of environmental setting and the staff that provide support, the "solutions" that have proved effective elsewhere may simply need minor modifications to provide insight into tried and true solutions. The RCA team should readily borrow from these industries and learn from their experiences.

Other Agencies, Programs and Providers. Team members who are conducting a RCA on behalf of a state or other large public agency can check with colleagues in other public agencies within their state that are also responsible for providing or overseeing support and service to persons with special needs (e.g., behavioral health, children, elderly, persons with ABI). Team members can ask whether or not these other agencies have had to address a similar type of issue (they probably have). Find out what they did to both correct and prevent future occurrences and whether or not their actions/interventions proved effective. Repeat the same process with other programs or providers if your RCA is being done at the provider/program level. Once again, try to learn from others. In a similar fashion, reach out to I/DD service systems in other states to learn about strategies they have found effective in reducing risk and addressing issues like the one that is the target of your RCA. Almost every state I/DD agency now operates a web site that provides contact information. Use this valuable resource. Learn from the experience of other states. To the extent possible, make prevention strategies and proposed solutions "evidence based."

ORGANIZE YOUR PREVENTION STRATEGIES

TOWARD THE END of the second meeting or at the beginning of the third and final RCA meeting the team leader should summarize findings and list all the potential solutions and prevention strategies that the team has identified to date. The information should be organized by aligning each strategy with its corresponding cause or cluster (group) of contributory factors. It can be helpful to visually illustrate these relationships using your Contributory Factors Diagram (if available) or by using "post-it" notes on a whiteboard.

Aligning Prevention Strategies and Contributory Factors

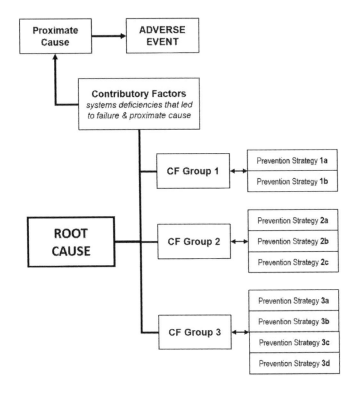

PRIORITIZE PREVENTION STRATEGIES

WHEN ALL OF THE POTENTIAL prevention strategies or solutions have been organized and given a priority they should be evaluated in terms of both their estimated impact and amount of effort that will be involved in implementing each of them. This can be done by assessing the potential effectiveness, feasibility and estimated cost of adopting each solution and/or barrier. Approaches that are not very practical (e.g., have a significant cost, high probability of being resisted or have a very lengthy timeline) should be discarded and the remaining solutions should then be rank ordered. This process of prioritizing solutions will assist leadership in making more informed decisions regarding the most viable and feasible next steps.

DEVELOP RECOMMENDATIONS

FOLLOWING THE PROCESS of prioritization, the team should develop a basic set of recommendations that are based on the top solutions that have been selected for each of the clusters of contributory factors. These recommendations will be included in the final report that is issued to leadership. Recommendations should be succinct and practical and logically aligned with the root cause and major factors that the team determined were most responsible for leading to the adverse event that was reviewed.

CHAPTER 6
How to Conduct a Root Cause Analysis
Part III: Report and Follow-up

ONCE THE TEAM has reached general agreement on the contributory factors and root cause responsible for the adverse event and it has arrived at a series of risk mitigation and safety enhancement recommendations it is time to prepare a draft report. The report should include a summary of basic findings, rationale for the findings and suggested solutions. The report must be written with care as it will become an extremely important document for communicating with leadership and other involved individuals. It should be based on facts, reasoned considerations and always avoid placing blame. The purpose of the report is to educate, not form the basis for punishment or disciplinary action.

REPORT FORMAT

THERE IS NO ONE ideal format for structuring and writing a final RCA report. It can be based on traditional narrative or on a structured form that allows you to "fill-in" answers to a variety of specific questions – or a combination of both. **Appendix L** contains a sample Root Cause Analysis Report Form that can be used if the more structured reporting format is desired. [Note: a report form that can be completed on-line and then printed is available for enrollees of the internet based on-line course associated with this book.] If a narrative report format is desired, it can still be helpful for the team leader to complete the report form as this will help assure that all important issues and questions have been adequately addressed in the analysis.

Whatever method is selected for developing the report it should include, at a minimum, the following information:

1. General description of the adverse event (what happened, who did it happen to, where and when did it happen, and, if applicable, what service/support provider was involved).

2. Brief description of the purpose of the root cause analysis (e.g., "... a formal root cause analysis was requested by the agency director to help identify what factors contributed to the incident and how to best reduce the risk of any future such incidents ...").

3. Membership of the RCA team, including who was the identified leader.

4. Brief description of the proximate cause of the incident.

5. Statement regarding whether or not there was deviation from a required or expected sequence of events that took place immediately prior to, at the time of or immediately after the incident under review.

6. Description of the identified contributory factors grouped by general category and ranked in terms of importance. The rationale for selection of the factors should be included (i.e., a summary statement as to how they contributed to the adverse event). If there is a formal contributory factors diagram it should be attached as an addendum to the report. While not necessary, it can be informative to also include common factors that were not identified as responsible (i.e., those that the team ruled out). Comment regarding the following general categories of factors is recommended:

- Actions or omissions that represented human error
- Equipment (absence of, malfunctions, misuse)
- Staffing (regular staff or staff unfamiliar with the people or routine)
- Staffing levels (required or adequate number of staff)
- Staff skills and training related to the activity or process
- Inaccurate or ambiguous information
- Communication problems
- Environmental factors
- Organizational and leadership issues
- Policy and/or procedure problems
- Individual assessment or personal planning/program design issues

7. The root cause, if identified by the team. Include a rationale for why this cause is considered fundamental to the error that resulted in the adverse event.

8. Summary of corrective and preventive actions that have already been taken to address the incident and reduce the probability it will happen again. [It is important to recognize efforts that have taken place in order to strengthen the development of a culture of safety and reduce the impression that the RCA process is punitive in nature.]

9. Summary of potential strategies and "solutions" that were considered by the team, with recommendations prioritized according to estimated effectiveness and efficiency. Include special considerations that will need to be taken into account by leadership if they elect to implement any of the team's recommendations.

10. Summary of any special incidental findings that the team believes leadership should be made aware of for either future analysis or corrective action.

11. Signature of the team leader

It is often helpful to prepare a brief executive summary of the report that captures the main points and that can be used when presenting the results of the analysis to leadership within the organization. A sample format for such an Executive Summary is **included in Appendix M.**

REPORT REVIEW

THE TEAM LEADER should circulate the draft report to all team members for their review prior to submission to leadership. It is important to make sure the entire team has an opportunity to review and comment on the contents of the final report. If there are major concerns or if any recommended edits are contradictory, it may be necessary to either meet with those team members or call a brief team meeting to discuss concerns and arrive at a consensus before issuing the final report. To the extent possible, the team leader should seek consensus on the major findings of the analysis, especially those that revolve around sensitive issues or resulted in strong objections by one or more team members.

STEP 10: REPORT & FOLLOW-UP

THE TEAM LEADER is responsible for arranging a formal presentation to the organization's leadership regarding the results and findings from the root cause analysis. It is important to conduct a face-to-face meeting; simply forwarding the final report is not recommended.

In addition to the team leader, selected members of the RCA team can be invited to participate in the leadership meeting. Keeping the group small will allow for more focused dialogue, and therefore it is recommended that participation in the meeting be selective (i.e., not all members of the team should be present).

Roles and Responsibilities. It is important for leadership and the RCA leader to differentiate the different roles and responsibilities for the RCA team versus the organization's management. Failure to do this can lead to a variety of problems including:

1. Disappointment and frustration by the RCA team if recommendations are not adopted
2. Confusion regarding responsibility for agency follow-up
3. Failure to clearly identify what, if any of the team recommendations will be implemented
4. Failure to establish specific improvement targets
5. Lack of a plan to evaluate the impact of any changes that are implemented

It is strongly recommended that the team leader clarify the following roles and responsibilities to both the members of the RCA team and senior leadership of the organization.

RCA Team Responsibilities. The team is primarily responsible for analyzing the adverse event and providing recommendations re: the best strategies for reducing the risk of future like incidents. The team is NOT responsible for deciding what actions can or will be taken by the organization. The responsibility of the team is therefore to:

- Gather information and review the target event
- Analyze and identify what latent faults and human errors contributed to the incident under review
- Carefully study possible solutions and methods to prevent future incidents

- Provide a listing of prioritized recommendations, including the pros and cons for each
- Present findings and be available for technical assistance if requested by leadership

Agency Leadership Responsibilities. The senior management and leadership of the organization is responsible for reviewing the findings and deciding what, if any action(s) will be taken to address future risk. Agency leadership is NOT responsible for selecting or following all of the recommendations provided by the team since it is a basic responsibility of management to consider the many different demands being placed on the organization for use of limited resources. Therefore, leadership must make decisions regarding the relative cost vs. benefit to be accrued from the different actions being proposed by the RCA team against the context of all the priorities that must be addressed. The responsibility of leadership is therefore to:

- Carefully review the RCA findings
- Decide what actions to take, now and in the future
- Assign responsibilities for those actions
- Establish a plan that includes methods to track progress and measure change
- Communicate to the organization and its stakeholders what is going to be done and why
- Manage the change process

The Presentation of Findings. If possible, the presentation meeting should be scheduled for between 45 and 90 minutes. Less time than that will not allow adequate dialogue and review of the issues. More time than that and other collateral issues may be injected into the meeting which can only serve to divert attention from the adverse incident that was the focus of the RCA.

The team leader (and any other team members that are present) should be prepared to provide a verbal presentation supplemented by copies of the RCA Report and a brief one page summary of the incident, major findings and priority recommendations. It is strongly recommended that the team leader provide a very brief overview of the principles of RCA, particularly the focus on understanding why something happened and what system faults may have contributed to any mistakes or errors made by staff. This summary should try to emphasize the importance of not using the RCA as a means of discipline or sanctioning since such action can only serve to compromise open and honest information sharing by staff and service providers.

The presence of a one page "executive summary" is also recommended as it will facilitate the discussion and prevent the need for perusing the entire RCA report and attachments. **Appendix M** contains a format for developing such an executive summary. The presentation to leadership itself should focus on important facts, the rationale for your findings and the estimated effectiveness and efficiency of proposed solutions. The team leader should share any identified "issues" or problems with the priority recommendations (e.g., length of time to implement, potential costs, staff and/or provider resistance). Being honest and practical will serve to increase credibility and the potential for acceptance of the team's recommendations.

In addition to the information re: the RCA findings it can also be helpful to provide any incidental findings that were determined important for management to be aware of. When sharing incidental findings note that these issues were not directly causative of the incident reviewed by the team but could present special risks that should be more carefully reviewed and addressed in order to prevent other serious adverse events from taking place in the future.

Follow-up. During the meeting it is advisable to discuss with leadership the potential importance of developing a formal improvement plan to reduce risk of future incidents such as the one reviewed by the team. The plan should include some method for measuring progress and evaluating the effectiveness of any changes and organizational interventions. Notify leadership that selected members of the RCA team can be available to answer questions, clarify findings, present to other groups and, if desired, provide technical assistance to whomever is charged with responsibility for the development of an improvement plan. It is not recommended that the RCA team itself assume this latter responsibility (role conflict).

INCIDENTAL FINDINGS

SPECIAL CONCERNS and practices that could lead to errors or contribute to other types of system failures will usually be identified by the team and should be documented and included in a special section of the final RCA report. These are called *incidental findings*. They represent inefficient processes or activities that, although not directly related to the failure under review, nonetheless should be evaluated further by the organization for possible correction since they appear to have a relatively high probability of increasing risk of harm.

The team leader or team facilitator should make a separate list of incidental findings on a separate wall chart or document log during the RCA team meetings. Incidental findings should only be very briefly discussed in team meetings. The meeting facilitator should attempt to redirect discussion if too much time and energy begins to become focused on an incidental finding as it can easily distract attention away from the main focus of the analysis.

This process of noting non-contributory factors or issues should occur throughout all of the RCA meetings. As noted, it must be carefully managed so that the group does not become focused on collateral issues, despite their apparent importance. Noting that the incidental finding will be documented and shared with leadership can often help ease the discussion back to the issue under review.

SUMMARY

ROOT CAUSE ANALYSIS is one of many different tools that can be used to enhance the safety and quality of services and supports that are provided to individuals with developmental disabilities by both large and small organizations. It can be an extremely powerful tool to help discover the reasons for – the underlying cause(s) - of very serious adverse events that result in harm and that, unfortunately, seem to happen way too often to persons who rely on others for support. Root cause analysis is a very structured and analytic process that focuses on identifying why "bad things" happen. It does not emphasize or even try to place blame. Understanding what contributes to the errors made by people (staff) is the key to putting in place effective risk prevention solutions that can have a lasting impact on the safety and quality of life of those citizens who happen to have an intellectual and/or other developmental disability.

Professional, management, supervisory, direct support and oversight personnel working in the field of I/DD are strongly encouraged to learn more about and then use the technique of root cause analysis to strengthen their systems of risk management. It will be well worth the time and effort!

REFERENCES

CHAPTER 2

[1] Reason, J. (1998). *Human error*. New York: Cambridge University Press.

[2] Reason, J. (1998). Achieving a safe culture: theory and practice. *Work and Stress*, 12(3), p. 294.

[3] Marx, D. (2007). *Patient safety and "just culture."* Outcome Engineering. Presentation accessed April 1, 2015 at http://www.health.ny.gov/professionals/patients/patient_safety/conference/2007/docs/patient_safety_ and_the_just_culture.pdf

[4] Leape, L. & Berwick, D. M. (2005). Five years after "To Err is Human": What have we learned? *Journal of the American Medical Association*, 293(19), 2384-2390.

[5] Norman, D. (2002). *The design of everyday things, First Edition*. New York: Basic Books.

[6] Spath, P. (2000). *Error Reduction in Health Care: A Systems Approach to Improving Patient Safety*. San Francisco: Jossey-Bass.

[7] Botwinick, L., Bisognano, M., & Haraden, C. (2006). *Leadership guide to patient safety*. IHI Innovation Series. Institute for Healthcare Improvement. Available at: https://www.IHI.org

CHAPTER 3

[1] To see how RCA was used by NASA following the Columbia space shuttle disaster interested readers can review: Berger, B. (2003). *Columbia Report Faults NASA Culture, Government Oversight*. Space.com. Accessed at: http://www.space.com/19476-space-shuttle-columbia-disaster-

[2] Hirsch & Wallace. (2001). Hirsch, Kenneth A. and Wallace, Dennis, T. *Step by Step Guide to Effective Root Cause Analysis*. Opus Communications, Marblehead, MAoversight.html

[3] Doing What Counts. (2000). *Doing What Counts for Patient Safety. Federal Actions to Reduce Medical Errors and their Impact.* Washington D.C. Report of the Quality Interagency Coordination Task Force, February, 2000.

[4] Institute of Medicine. (1999). *To Err is Human: Building a Safer Health System*. Washington D.C. National Academy Press.

[5] NPSF. (2014). *Creating a world where patients and those who care for them are free from harm*. National Patient Safety Foundation. Available at: http://www.npsf.org

APPENDICES

Appendix A

How Strong is Your Organization's Culture of Safety?

Effective and meaningful risk management requires the presence of an organizational culture of safety and a "readiness" to consistently use structured and analytic tools to identify problems and take action to prevent future adverse events.

Carefully review the following statements to assess your organization's readiness to implement a truly comprehensive approach to risk management and its culture of safety. Check those characteristics that apply to your organization now. Think about how you can address "**obstacles**" or "**barriers**" to establishing a meaningful culture of safety that you have identified. Laying the proper "groundwork" will help make your efforts to promote safety and mitigate risk of harm within your organization much easier and more effective.

☐ Leadership tends to avoid the active identification of problems that may compromise safety and waits until something bad happens before acting.

☐ When an adverse event does take place leadership usually "points the finger" and tries to blame staff for making a mistake.

☐ It is unusual for my organization to analyze and use data about adverse incidents to target areas for risk mitigation.

☐ Managers and supervisors within my organization rarely focus on trying to understand why a problem has taken place, especially when the reason may be faulty management decisions or poorly designed organizational systems.

☐ Leadership and managers/supervisors typically do not communicate with front line staff and make decisions about safety in isolation (i.e., without the active involvement of staff).

☐ Managers and supervisors do not actively seek out feedback from staff and consumers concerning what they can do to improve safety and quality within the organization.

☐ There are very few or no formal written policies and guidelines regarding the use of risk management tools such as risk screening, root cause analysis, mortality review, incident reporting and/or failure mode and effects analysis. What policies exist, are not widely understood nor used on a regular basis by staff within the organization.

☐ Our organizational "culture" (its traditional way of responding to incidents) usually focuses on minimizing exposure to negative criticism or potential litigation.

☐ In general, there is not very much teamwork within my work unit or organization.

☐ My organization does not have a formal and written safety plan.

☐ There is no risk management policy or entity (e.g., staff, committee) assigned to focus on the reduction of risk and improvement of safety within my organization.

☐ Leadership within my organization seems to be more concerned with covering up or hiding problems rather than finding or fixing them.

☐ My organization typically does not focus on preventing harm to people but rather emphasizes punishing those who may be responsible for the harm.

☐ When someone is hurt or suffers from an "avoidable" death my organization usually goes for a "quick fix" that does not really correct any systemic issues or problems.

☐ Most staff would agree that our organization does not try to learn from mistakes and errors.

☐ Most staff are afraid they will be disciplined if they make a mistake or report that an adverse event almost took place in their workplace.

☐ When something "bad" happens, my organization tries to find a solution only by talking with people within the agency and does not usually seek information from outside sources (e.g., other agencies, other industries) on possible corrective and preventive strategies.

☐ Professional and clinical staff do not pay attention to or seek out input from direct support staff when it comes to designing programs or identifying risks.

☐ My organization does not have a culture that seeks constant improvement, but rather only implements change when it is forced to.

☐ My organization does not share or publish the results of data analyses and aggregate analytic reviews (i.e., share findings and results from mortality and incident reporting with staff, service recipients and the public at large).

☐ OTHER Barrier:

Number of Obstacles/Barriers: _____

READINESS PLAN: Summarize the top 3 barriers that may be interfering with establishing a true culture of safety within your organization. Note how these could be effectively addressed, who would be best to work on the change and how you would know when the issue was resolved.

Obstacle 1:

_____

How it will be addressed:

_____
_____
_____

Who will do it: _____ Timeline: _____

Readiness Indicator(s):

_____
_____

Obstacle 2:

_____

How it will be addressed:

_____
_____
_____

Who will do it: _____ Timeline: _____

Readiness Indicator(s):

_____
_____

Obstacle 3:

_____

How it will be addressed:

_____
_____
_____

Who will do it: _____ Timeline: _____

Readiness Indicator(s):

_____
_____

APPENDIX B

How Ready is Your Organization for RCA?

Root Cause Analysis (RCA) is a structured analytic process that attempts to uncover systems factors that may be setting the stage for human errors that can result in adverse events. RCA can be perceived as "threatening" to individuals within an organization. In order for it to be accepted and effective, RCA requires the presence of a true "culture of safety" and organizational "readiness" to assertively explore and correct individual and systems issues that are contributing to errors and failures that cause adverse events.

Carefully review the following statements to assess your organization's readiness for RCA. Check those that apply to your organization. Think about how you can address the "obstacles" that you have identified and develop a plan to overcome organizational resistance. Remember that establishing the proper "groundwork" will expedite the use of RCA and make your job much easier and more effective.

- ☐ A formal RCA has never been performed within your organization and most members of the organization are <u>not</u> familiar with the process.

- ☐ Senior leadership of your organization is not aware of the benefits of RCA as a risk mitigation tool and/or most managers have not been introduced to the process of RCA.

- ☐ Managers and supervisors have not been notified by senior leadership that RCA is a preferred method for improving safety within your organization and is to be supported.

- ☐ There is no formal policy regarding the use of RCA.

- ☐ Your organizational "culture" (traditional way of responding to incidents) usually focuses on minimizing exposure to negative criticism.

- ☐ Staff and union representatives have not been oriented to the basic focus of RCA as a non-punitive approach to improving quality and safety that emphasizes correcting systems failures and not "blaming" people.

- ☐ It is unusual for your organization to use analytic methods – including the analysis of data and post-incident reviews – to correct problems and improve performance.

- ☐ The first reaction of managers and supervisors is to "point the finger" and "blame" individuals when adverse events take place.

- ☐ Your organization does not have a consistent and structured approach to improving safety – there is no visible safety plan.

- ☐ There is no formal risk management policy or entity (e.g., staff, committee) assigned to focus on the reduction of risk and improvement of safety within your organization.

PLAN to Address Obstacles:

APPENDIX C

Sequence Analysis Form

Organization:

Date:

Incident Under Review:

RCA Team Leader:

Sequence Analysis Prepared by:

Date	Time (Approximate)	Who	What Happened (The Event or Activity)	Ref Document

Date	Time (Approximate)	Who	What Happened (The Event or Activity)	Ref Document

Continue with additional pages if needed

Notes:

APPENDIX D

EXAMPLE

Partially Completed Sequence Analysis for Drowning Incident

Date	Time (Approximate)	Who	What Happened (The Event or Activity)	Ref Document
5/7	3:20 P	S1, S2 All 4 residents	Residents & 2 staff arrive home from day program and enter house. Go into living room in wheelchairs – outdoor clothing removed and hung up.	Inv Rep 1
	3:30 P	GH Spvsr	GH Spvsr (on site) takes call from parent.- after 5 min instructs staff to begin bathing routine	Inv Rep 1
	3:40 P	S1, S2	KE escorted to bathroom by 2 staff. KE assisted undressing to prepare for bath	Inv Rep 1
	3:48 P	S1, S2	KE put in lift by S1 & S2	Intrvw 2
	3:50 P	GH Spvsr	Spvsr observes KE in lift but not yet in tub	Intrvw 1
	3:52 P	S1, S2	KE placed into tub chair by S1 & S2; straps not yet attached according to S2	Inv Rep 1 Intrvw 3
	3:54 P	GH Spvsr	Spvsr gets phone call – problem with staff scheduling – 5 min call	Intrvw 1
	3:55 P	S1	S1 leaves bathroom	Intrvw 3
	3:56 P	S1	HM reports that S1 goes to Living Room to assist another resident	Intrvw 3
	3:58 P	S2	KE lowered into water in tub	Inv Rep 1
	4:00 P	S1, GH Spvsr	GH Spvsr asks S1 to prepare meds for 2 residents	Intrvw 3
	4:03 P	S2	S2 leaves bathroom to get towel – states he was gone for only a "few minutes"	Inv Rep 1 Intrvw 2
	4:03 P	GH Spvsr	Spvsr goes to kitchen area to check on S1 and then goes back to living room	Intrvw 1
	4:05 P	S2	S2 returns to bathroom and sees KE under water with "bubbles from mouth"	Inv Rep 1

Sequence should be continued – description of events that follow using the same format

APPENDIX E
Risk Management in DD

Checklist for RCA Team Leader

Meeting Preparation

- ☐ Review of all pertinent documents with copies for team members
  - ☐ Incident Report(s)
  - ☐ Investigation Report(s)
  - ☐ Supporting Documents (e.g., interviews, emergency response reports)
  - ☐ RCA Report Form
- ☐ Sequence Analysis completed and printed with copies for team members
- ☐ Flowcharts completed and printed with copies for team members
- ☐ Summary document for orientation to RCA
- ☐ List of Meeting Rules & Principles
- ☐ Team member assignment and notification of meeting schedule and location
- ☐ Meeting materials (e.g., handouts, flip-charts, optional computer and projector)

First Meeting

- ☐ Introductions and expected roles
- ☐ Summary of the purpose of the RCA
- ☐ Brief orientation to the process of RCA
- ☐ Review of RCA Report Form (to illustrate expected outcomes)
- ☐ Review of the target incident/adverse event
- ☐ Review Sequence Analysis and Flowcharts of the incident
- ☐ Compare to best practices and/or written protocols/procedures
- ☐ Identify critical errors
- ☐ (Optional) Classify each of the errors by type
- ☐ Review Contributory Factors Checklist
- ☐ Identify Contributory Factors - brainstorming
- ☐ Drill down to second and third level Contributory Factors
- ☐ Seek consensus on most important Contributory Factors
- ☐ Make assignments (homework)
- ☐ Verify next meeting

Second Meeting

- ☐ Review any revisions to the sequence analysis
- ☐ Review identified Contributory Factors
- ☐ Seek input and ideas re: additional Contributory Factors
- ☐ Group Contributory Factors
- ☐ Develop Contributory Factors Diagram (hierarchy)
- ☐ Optional: Complete first section of Root Cause Analysis Report Form
- ☐ IF TIME: Begin review of solutions and barriers
- ☐ Make assignments (literature review, checking with other agency personnel or resources re: potential strategies, etc.)
- ☐ Verify next meeting

Third Meeting

- ☐ Review potential solutions and barriers – review ideas generated through literature and experience of others
- ☐ Review potential solutions and barriers – brainstorming
- ☐ Select priority solutions
- ☐ Evaluate priority solutions for effectiveness and efficiency
- ☐ Identify corrective and preventive actions already taken
- ☐ Select solutions that will be recommended to leadership
- ☐ Identify and document important incidental findings
- ☐ Complete Root Cause Analysis Report Form
- ☐ Notify team members of plans for sharing draft report and seeking approval
- ☐ Notify team members of plans for reviewing findings with leadership

Report Preparation

- ☐ Prepare draft report using RCA Report Form or Narrative format
- ☐ Distribute to team members for review and comment
- ☐ Make necessary edits and changes
- ☐ (Optional) Prepare formal flowchart for attachment
- ☐ (Optional) Prepare contributory factors diagram for attachment

Communication with Leadership

- ☐ Schedule meeting with leadership
- ☐ Provide brief orientation re: purpose of RCA and "do's and don'ts" for agency action
- ☐ Provide written one page summary and full report with attachments
- ☐ Verbally review major findings and recommendations
- ☐ Clarify any additional team activity requested by leadership
- ☐ Notify team members of reaction of leadership and any planned actions
- ☐ Maintain formal official file of documents and reports

NOTES:

RCA Meeting Rules & Principles

Root Cause Analysis is a structured analytic process designed to identify why an adverse event has taken place and what can be done to reduce the probability that this same type of incident will occur in the future. The following "Meeting Rules and Principles" are designed to facilitate the analysis and allow the RCA process to proceed in an effective fashion.

1. Focus on the **FACTS** and avoid injecting bias, opinion and assumptions into your review.

2. Keep it **POSITIVE**. Do not place blame. Avoid derogatory statements when reviewing the actions of persons involved in an incident.

3. Emphasize **CAUSAL STATEMENTS** that will identify WHY something happened. Always describe the "cause and effect" relationship and why something led to a mistake.

4. Keep **DRILLING DOWN** to uncover the most fundamental reason or cause. Do this by repeatedly asking "why?"

5. There should always be a **PRECEDING CAUSE** for all human errors. Do not simply identify the error as it is the <u>cause</u> of the error, not the error itself, that will generate productive solutions

6. Focus on what **CONTRIBUTED** to or caused a procedural deviation, not just the deviation itself. When a deviation from expected practice does occur you must try to understand <u>why</u> the person did not follow the procedure or plan.

7. Avoid **NEGATIVE DESCRIPTORS** and shorthand explanations (e.g., "inadequate," "insufficient," "poorly designed") and describe why.

8. Remember, all team members are **EQUALS** and must have an opportunity to contribute to the discussion. Do not defer to certain team members.

9. **ASK QUESTIONS** if you are not sure. Never assume everyone else understands. Avoid making assumptions.

10. Look **OUTSIDE** for answers and ideas for solutions. Take the time to review the literature and learn how others have addressed similar problems.

APPENDIX G
Risk Management in DD

COMMON FACTORS CHECKLIST
Factors that Contribute to Adverse Events for People with I/DD

When attempting to identify what may have caused or contributed to an adverse event or system failure in a program or service system that supports people with a developmental disability, make sure you consider the following factors. Place a checkmark next to each factor that you believe may have been present and therefore influenced or caused the adverse incident or failure. Use the last column for notes that will help you remember why you identified a factor as relevant. Add additional factors that you and the team believe are important for understanding why the adverse event took place. You can use the headings to help organize contributory factors into related clusters or groupings when you develop your contributory factors diagram and write your RCA report.

1. STAFF FACTORS

Check (✓) if Relevant	Contributory Factor	Description	NOTES
☐	Workload	The number of staff present to carry out the assigned duties in the expected timelines was not present. The amount of required work was not consistent with the duties and assigned tasks for available staff.	
☐	Awareness	Staff and other support personnel were not aware of what tasks they needed to do and when those tasks had to be performed. Staff did not know what to do.	
☐	Staff Skills	Staff and other support personnel did not have the necessary skills or knowledge to perform the assigned duties in a safe and appropriate manner. Staff did not know how to perform the required tasks.	
☐	Experience	Staff did not have the necessary experience performing the task. If not experienced, they did not know whom to access for direction and support.	
☐	Prioritization	Staff or supervisors did not set priorities for multiple tasks and responsibilities. The "assumed" priorities were not consistent with needs, policy or agency expectations.	
☐	Time Allocation	Staff or supervisors/management did not set aside sufficient time to perform priority tasks within the established and expected timeline(s).	
☐	Working with Others	Staff were not aware of whom they needed to work with as a team to perform certain tasks.	

Check (✓) if Relevant	Contributory Factor	Description	NOTES
		Staff and other support personnel did not effectively collaborate when necessary.	
☐	Relationship with Other Staff	Staff did not have positive relationships with other personnel. Conflicts and/or relationship issues interfered with the ability of staff to properly perform tasks in a safe and/or efficient manner.	
☐	Relationships with Service Recipients	Staff did not have a positive and supportive relationship with the people they were assisting. Staff or other support personnel had negative attitudes toward or opinions about one or more service recipients.	
☐	Motivation	Staff did not have incentives for performing the required activity correctly. The task was considered unimportant by staff or it was not recognized by the organization as important. There were no clear consequences for completing or not completing the activity.	
☐	Other:	[Describe]	

2. SERVICE RECIPIENT FACTORS

Check (✓) if Relevant	Contributory Factor	Description	NOTES
☐	Adherence	Persons receiving support did not adhere to support plans on a consistent basis or were not provided with effective prompts and other supports to assure compliance with critical aspects of their care.	
☑	Awareness	Persons receiving support were not aware of what tasks they needed to do and when those tasks were to be performed.	
☐	Skills	Persons receiving support did not have the necessary skills or knowledge to perform the assigned duties in a safe and appropriate manner. They did not know how to perform the required tasks. Adequate and effective skills training was not provided.	
☐	Experience	Persons receiving support were placed in a novel or unique situation. He or she was not familiar with the demands and risks of the situation.	

Check (✓) if Relevant	Contributory Factor	Description	NOTES
☐	Cognitive Ability	Persons receiving support did not have the cognitive skills necessary to understand and complete required critical care activities when and if direct staff support was not available.	
☐	Physical Ability	Persons receiving support did not have the physical ability to prevent the incident without staff or other support. They did not have the physical ability to perform the task safely.	
☐	Communication Ability	Persons receiving support were not able to communicate needs and concerns that required staff assistance or intervention. Alternative and assistive communication systems or training were not present to assure individuals could communicate with one another.	
☐	Disease Complexity/Acuity	The medical and health status of the person receiving support was complex and required close monitoring or specialized care. The condition had rapid onset.	
☐	Supervision	The persons receiving support had a level of need for support that required the presence of supervision or observation during the activity that was not provided.	
☐	Relationships with Others	The person receiving support did not have a positive relationship with others (other service recipients, staff, community members, etc.). The individual exhibited aggressive or dangerous behaviors towards others.	
☐	Other:	[Describe]	
☐	Other:	[Describe]	

3. ASSESSMENT & PLANNING

Check (✓) if Relevant	Contributory Factor	Description	NOTES
☐	Behavioral Assessment & Support	Proper behavioral assessment, including risk to self or others, was not present or was inadequate. Specialized behavior management or treatment services were not provided in a timely or adequate fashion.	
☐	Medical Assessment & Care	A complete medical and health assessment was not conducted. Necessary supplemental tests were not performed. Medical factors that posed risks were not identified or addressed. Specialized medical services were not provided in a timely or adequate fashion.	
☐	Physical Assessment	A physical assessment (including contraband search) was not conducted properly. Physical limitations and/or threats were not identified.	
☐	Planning	A timely and complete planning process was not conducted for the person or persons receiving support. The planning process did not include all required and essential components.	
☐	Risk Screening & Planning	An assessment of personal risks that require special attention in the individual support plan was not conducted. Identified risks were not properly addressed in the support plan.	
☐	Participation	The support and service planning process did not include sufficient knowledgeable people. Active participation by the service recipient and his/her advocates and surrogates was not present.	
☐	Timeliness	The assessment or planning process was not conducted in a timely fashion. Essential services or follow-up evaluations were not provided in a timely fashion.	
☐	Other:	[Describe]	
☐	Other:	[Describe]	

4. COMMUNICATION

Check (✓) if Relevant	Contributory Factor	Description	NOTES
☐	With Service Recipient	Staff and other support personnel did not have good communication with the person receiving support. Lack of adequate communication hindered awareness of a problem.	
☐	With Family	There was inadequate or poor communication with the family or other knowledgeable persons. Poor communication reduced staff awareness of issues or risks.	
☐	Inadequate Information - Special Needs	Staff and other personnel who provided care or services did not possess adequate information re: special risks, concerns or needs of the person(s) receiving support. The record was incomplete. Inadequate documentation was present.	
☐	Inadequate Information and/or Procedures	Staff and other support personnel did not have access to clear information regarding proper procedures, protocols or practices. Information, if available, was confusing, contradictory or difficult to locate.	
☐	Identification	Proper service recipient identification procedures were not present.	
☐	Other:	[Describe]	
☐	Other:	[Describe]	

5. EQUIPMENT & SUPPLIES

Check (✓) if Relevant	Contributory Factor	Description	NOTES
☐	Poor Maintenance	Necessary equipment was not well maintained. Equipment was broken or did not operate properly due to lack of maintenance.	
☐	Defective	Equipment was not properly designed or had defects. The equipment was not assembled properly. Equipment was not used as intended.	
☐	Not Available or Inadequate	Adapted or other necessary equipment was not available or was inadequate to the needs of the person(s) receiving support.	
☐	Inadequate Signage	Posted instructions or warnings were not available or located properly. High risk areas or activities did not have adequate signage to	

Check (✓) if Relevant	Contributory Factor	Description	NOTES
		prompt individuals and staff of dangers.	
☐	Medication Control	Medication was not properly controlled or stored. Access to medication was faulty.	
☐	Food Control	Access to food and other edible items was not properly controlled. Food was not stored properly.	
☐	Potency of Medication	The potency of medication was compromised and/or medication had exceeded its expiration date.	
☐	Poor Labeling	Medications or other equipment or supplies were not labeled properly. Labels were confusing or incomplete.	
☐	Other:	[Describe]	
☐	Other:	[Describe]	

6. ENVIRONMENT

Check (✓) if Relevant	Contributory Factor	Description	NOTES
☐	Safety Codes	The physical environment did not meet established or required building or safety codes or standards.	
☐	Improper Use	The physical environment was not designed or intended for the use to which it was put.	
☐	Distraction	The environment was noisy and contained distractions that compromised the ability of staff to attend properly to tasks.	
☐	Clutter	The environment was cluttered and impeded safe ambulation or movement.	
☐	Line of Sight	The environment did not allow for needed line of sight to assure ongoing observation.	
☐	Handicapped Accessible	The environment was not handicapped accessible and did not contain needed adaptations.	
☐	Novelty	The person(s) receiving support was placed in a novel or unique situation. He or she was not familiar with the demands and risks of the situation.	
☐	Supervision	The service recipients' need for support required the presence of supervision during the	

Check (✓) if Relevant	Contributory Factor	Description	NOTES
		activity or event that was not recognized or provided.	
☐	Emergency Procedures	There were inadequate emergency procedures immediately available to staff. There was no emergency plan present to guide staff. Emergency numbers were not posted.	
☐	Other:	[Describe]	
☐	Other:	[Describe]	

7. POLICIES & PROCEDURES

Check (✓) if Relevant	Contributory Factor	Description	NOTES
☐	No Policy	There was no formal written policy or procedure governing the activity. Staff were not able to reference agency guidelines or protocols.	
☐	Contradictory Policy	Policies and procedures were inconsistent and contradictory. Verbal instruction was different from procedural requirements. Policies and procedures were not updated to reflect changes in actual practice.	
☐	Inadequate Policy	Policies and procedures were not complete, did not meet regulatory requirements, or were inconsistent with established standards and best practice expectations. Policies and procedures were not clear or concise.	
☐	Communication and Awareness	There was inadequate communication re: new policy requirements. Staff and others were not aware of changes or revisions to policy or procedure.	
☐	Employee Screening	There were inadequate policy requirements for screening employees. Individuals with established histories of behavior that could compromise safety and quality of care – including abuse and neglect - were working with service recipients without special protections.	
☐	Training	There were inadequate policy requirements for training. Staff were not required by policy to meet any minimum training requirements or to	

Check (✓) if Relevant	Contributory Factor	Description	NOTES
		demonstrate competency.	
☐	Fiscal Control	There were inadequate or inconsistent policy requirements for the management and control of consumer funds.	
☐	Assessment	There were inadequate policy requirements for proper assessment of service recipient health, behavior, and other critical support needs and preferences.	
☐	Planning	There were inadequate policy requirements for proper support planning and revision of supports based on changing needs.	
☐	Monitoring	There were inadequate policy requirements for monitoring services and supports to assure they were safe, meeting critical needs, and provided in accordance with individual support plans.	
☐	Documentation	There were inadequate policy requirements for creating, documenting and maintaining service recipient records, including standards for protecting privacy. There were no written policy requirements for sharing essential information with external service providers and clinicians.	
☐	Other:	[Describe]	
☐	Other:	[Describe]	

8. ORGANIZATIONAL & LEADERSHIP FACTORS

Check (✓) if Relevant	Contributory Factor	Description	NOTES
☐	Culture	The organizational culture did not emphasize safety or adherence to established standards. The culture did not support continuous improvement.	
☐	Identification of Safety Hazards	The organization did not encourage and actively support the identification of problems and hazards by front line personnel. There was no mechanism for service recipients and family members to communicate concerns about safety and quality of care.	
☐	Availability of Leaders	Leaders and managers were not available to personnel. There were no established methods for communicating with senior leaders.	
☐	Structure	The table of organization or command structure was not clear. Staff were confused about who was responsible for what.	
☐	Intimidation & Blaming	There was an atmosphere of intimidation in the organization that hindered open communication. Staff perceived the presence of negative consequences for communicating problems or issues that required the attention of leadership or provision of resources. Senior management typically engaged in blaming staff for mistakes rather than seeking out problems with the support structure or system.	
☐	Other:	[Describe]	
☐	Other:	[Describe]	

REMEMBER: In the preliminary stages of analysis always keep an open mind. Explore all possibilities. It is important to consider "suspected" or "probable" causes. It is not necessary to establish "proof" or determine whether or not any specific factor was definitely responsible for an error or failure when first identifying contributory factors. Make sure your team recognizes that a variety of issues can set the stage for human error and equipment failures. Identifying and addressing the most important of these will be essential for establishing the most effective strategies for the prevention of similar adverse events in the future.

S.D. Staugaitis

IMPORTANT FACTORS FOR REVIEW:

Note below the most important causative and contributory factors that should be addressed in your analysis of the adverse event under review:

BRAINSTORMING PRINCIPLES
How to Encourage the Generation of Creative Ideas

Brainstorming is a widely used technique for generating a large number of ideas within a group of people. It requires an atmosphere of uninhibited and open discussion, where team members feel free to share even improbable ideas. Because brainstorming is very different from the usual process of analysis and discussion that takes place in a group, it is essential that the team leader explain the rules for brainstorming and note when the process is to begin and end.

RULES for Brainstorming:

1. **Suspend Judgments** – team members must not criticize or point out problems with other people's ideas.
2. **Free Thinking** – participants need to allow themselves to drift or freewheel. The group should encourage and support wild and even silly ideas.
3. **More is Better** – in the beginning you want to generate a large number of ideas. Encourage members to keep throwing out ideas quickly.
4. **Cross-fertilize** – participants should build upon the ideas of other members. Encourage slightly different "takes" on any given idea. Remember, the group owns the ideas, not any individual.

STAGES of Brainstorming:

1. **State the Problem.** First, the team leader should state the problem or issue (e.g., "What factors could have led to John leaving Jim alone").
2. **Clarify the Problem.** Second, ask team members to restate the problem or issue using different words. After you have a number of alternatives, have the group select the one they believe will generate the best ideas.
3. **Generate Ideas.** The third step involves the brainstorming itself. Write down all of the ideas. Encourage members to open up and think freely. No discussion or criticism of any specific idea is allowed at this stage. Once this step is completed (usually about 10 to 15minutes), go to the fourth and final stage.
4. **Evaluate Ideas.** During this last stage the group should briefly discuss all the ideas. Those that appear least promising should be eliminated (consensus decision). Then prioritize the remaining ideas. The highest priority ideas can then be documented.

The technique of brainstorming is especially useful when conducting a Root Cause Analysis (RCA) or a Failure Mode and Effects Analysis (FMEA) to encourage your team to think "freely" and to identify <u>all</u> possible causes for error and failure; and, to assure the team does not overlook potentially effective solutions that can be used to prevent similar failures from taking place in the future. Therefore, use the technique of brainstorming to "think out of the box" so your team can better understand the full scope of issues that may impact risk and to make sure team members fully explore both conventional and unconventional strategies for improvement.

7 COMMON REASONS FOR STAFF ERROR

When thinking about possible causes consider the following seven (7) common reasons for staff (and others) to experience errors and potential factors that may contribute to each type of error. Note that many of the potential contributory factors are really latent faults related to organizational issues. Such latent faults set the stage for later active errors by staff. Once identified, the organization should consider ways to correct them in order to reduce the probability the same types of active errors by staff will occur in the future. The 7 Common Reasons for Staff Error are:

1. **Person doesn't know WHAT to do.** This is a knowledge-based error and can be caused by any number of factors including:

    a. Incomplete instructions/policy/procedure

    b. Confusing or contradictory instructions/procedures

    c. Instructions that are too general and not specific to the person being supported

    d. Reading levels that are too advanced

    e. Inadequate communication

    f. Afraid to ask questions

    g. Routines are confusing or not posted

    h. No training or training was incomplete or not competency based

    i. Information overload – must learn too many different tasks too quickly

    j. Person placed in a new situation and is not familiar with the people, their needs, routines, programs, etc.

2. **Person doesn't know HOW to do it.** This is a skill-based error that can be influenced by all of the factors identified above in no. 1 and also:

    a. Using new or novel equipment

    b. No demonstration of how something is done

    c. Task doesn't occur very often – long period of time since it was last done

    d. Instructions are not readily available or are confusing

    e. No other person available to demonstrate the task

    f. Training material was complex and not based on "hands on" demonstration

    g. Minimal or no opportunity to practice the task under supervision

    h. No supervisory feedback on task performance

3. **Person doesn't know WHY they should do it.** This is an awareness-based error that can have many different causes including:

   a. Lack "big picture" and an understanding of related consequences if something is not done properly

   b. Risk seems too general - not personalized

   c. Risk is viewed as highly unlikely – too rare to be concerned about

   d. Believe their situation is different from others

   e. No prior experience with the risk or consequences

   f. Don't believe it really matters if the task is done differently

   g. Co-workers and supervisors have not stressed the importance of doing the task a certain way

4. **Person FORGETS to do it.** This is a knowledge and/or skill-based error that can be caused by:

   a. Environments that are too "busy" and where activities are "rushed"

   b. Distractions in the environment

   c. Numerous competing demands and activities

   d. Intervening responsibilities/tasks – e.g., suddenly become sidetracked with another service recipient

   e. Limited or No visible cues or prompts that can serve as reminders

   f. Absence of checklists or other "memory aids"

   g. Overly complex instructions or program requirements

5. **Person lacks necessary RESOURCES to do it.** This is often an organization-based error (latent error) that is not uncommon in high-demand DD programs and that can be caused by:

   a. Not enough staff on duty for type of activity

   b. Inadequate, broken or antiquated equipment

   c. Limited supplies and materials

   d. Limited supervision or technical assistance

6. **Person has insufficient TIME to do it.** This too is an organization-based error that can be caused by:

   a. Too many activities/tasks scheduled for a limited time period

   b. Inconsistent work schedule

   c. Routines are not standardized or structured

7. **Person doesn't WANT to do it.** This is a motivation-based error that can be caused by a very wide variety of factors including but not limited to:

    a. Receive little or no recognition for the activity

    b. Task is unpleasant or boring

    c. Task requires more effort and takes more time than other ways of doing something

    d. Task can lead to embarrassment or injury

    e. History of being criticized or "punished" if they make a mistake

    f. Interferes with more desirable activities

    g. Want to avoid interactions with others involved in task

The identified "reason(s)" will determine what "solutions" should be considered to reduce the probability the same type of error will take place in the future.

APPENDIX J
EXAMPLE OF AN AFFINITY DIAGRAM

Headings →
(reflect general theme)

STAFFING ISSUES

POLICIES & PROCEDURES

ENVIRONMENT

1ˢᵗ **Level Contributory Factors**
(causes or reasons for any errors that led to the adverse event)

STAFFING ISSUES	POLICIES & PROCEDURES	ENVIRONMENT
Training was only verbal with no hands-on practice	Policy was not updated	Distracting environment at pick-up time
Different staff used for transport – had limited experience	Procedure too general & not specific for different vehicles, lifts and WCs	Pressure on staff to move people quickly
No supervisory observation of procedure	No visual cues or instructions available	
2ⁿᵈ staff member not available outside to assist on lift		

APPENDIX K

ILLUSTRATION OF THE HIERARCHY FOR
A CONTRIBUTORY FACTORS DIAGRAM

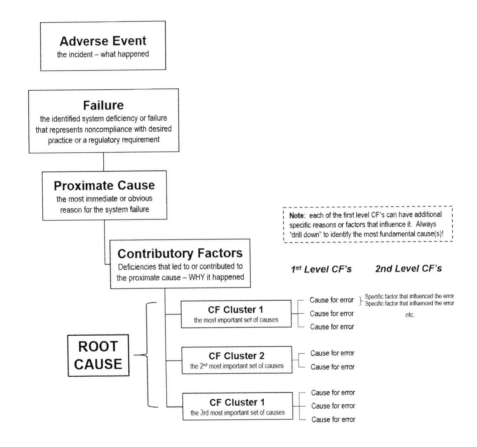

ROOT CAUSE ANALYSIS REPORT FORM[1]

Complete this form to document the findings of the Root Cause Analysis. The form can be completed during or after the RCA meeting(s) by a designated team member. Prior to submission to the organization's leadership the RCA team leader should provide all team members with a draft for review and comment.

IDENTIFYING INFORMATION regarding the adverse event.	
State or Region/Area:	PUBLIC AGENCY responsible for oversight/funding:
Responsible Service Provider:	Program/Facility or Location where incident took place:
If an individual service recipient experienced significant harm, list initials or ID No.:	City/Town (Location of program/facility):
If other individuals experienced harm, provide either their Service Recipient ID No. or their Initials:	RCA Team Members: Team Leader:

THE EVENT – Briefly describe what happened and any harm that resulted. Identify the proximate cause, if known.

Description:

What type of major harm did the incident result in: ☐ None ☐ Death ☐ Serious Injury ☐ Significant property damage ☐ Significant financial loss ☐ Other:

BACKGROUND & EXPECTED SEQUENCE – Answer the following questions (brief summary only) and attach supporting documents where appropriate.

---

[1] Adapted from a template utilized by the Australian Department of Human Services for use by Health Care Organizations and Hospitals. [see http://www.health.vic.gov.au/clinrisk/investigation/root-cause-analysis.htm for more information]

Was there a specific sequence of events that was expected to take place (e.g., written procedure, individual program)? ☐ Yes ☐ No ☐ Not Known	Briefly describe what was expected to take place. [Attach a flowchart if available.]
Was there a deviation from the expected sequence? ☐ Yes ☐ No ☐ Not Known	If YES, briefly describe the deviation. [Attach flowchart if available.]
Was any deviation from the expected sequence likely to have led to or contributed to the adverse event? ☐ Yes ☐ No ☐ Not Known	If YES, describe how the deviation contributed to the adverse event.
Was the expected sequence described in policy, procedure, written guidelines, or included in staff training? ☐ Yes ☐ No ☐ Not Known	If Yes, what was the source?
Optional: Does the expected sequence or process meet regulatory requirements and/or practice standards? ☐ Yes ☐ No ☐ Not Known	If YES, cite references and/or literature reviewed by the team. If NO, describe any major deviation from requirements or practice standards.

OTHER INFORMATION: Briefly describe any additional information regarding the sequence of events that is important for understanding what took place and how it related to expectations and/or standards.

CONTRIBUTORY FACTORS SUMMARY - Answer the following questions (brief summary only) and attach supporting documents where appropriate.	
Did **human action** or inaction appear to	If YES, briefly describe the actions (or

contribute to the adverse event? ☐ Yes ☐ No ☐ Not Known	inactions) and how they contributed.
Did a defect, malfunction, misuse of, or absence of **equipment** appear to contribute to the event? ☐ Yes ☐ No ☐ Not Known	If YES, describe what equipment was involved and how it appeared to contribute.
Was the procedure or activity involved in the event being carried out in the usual **location**? ☐ Yes ☐ No ☐ Not Known	If NO, describe where and why a different location was utilized and how that contributed to the adverse event.
Was the procedure or activity being carried out by **regular staff** familiar with the consumer and activity? ☐ Yes ☐ No ☐ Not Known	If NO, describe who was carrying out the activity and why regular staff was not involved.
Was staff credentialed, skilled and properly **trained** to carry out the tasks expected of them? ☐ Yes ☐ No ☐ Not Known	If NO, describe.
Were **staffing levels** consistent with expectations and considered to have been adequate at the time of the incident? ☐ Yes ☐ No ☐ Not Known	If NO, describe why.
Were there **other staffing factors** identified as responsible for or contributing to the adverse event? ☐ Yes ☐ No ☐ Not Known	If YES, describe those other staffing factors.

Did inaccurate or ambiguous **information** contribute to or cause the adverse event? ☐ Yes ☐ No ☐ Not Known	If YES, describe what information and how it contributed.
Did a lack of communication or incomplete **communication** contribute to or cause the adverse event? ☐ Yes ☐ No ☐ Not Known	If YES, describe who and what and how it contributed.
Did any **environmental** factors contribute to or cause the adverse event? ☐ Yes ☐ No ☐ Not Known	If YES, describe what factors and how they contributed.
Did any **organizational** or leadership factors contribute to or cause the adverse event? ☐ Yes ☐ No ☐ Not Known	If YES, describe what factors and how they contributed.
Did factors related to **policy and procedure**s contribute to the adverse event? ☐ Yes ☐ No ☐ Not Known	If YES, what policies/procedures and how they contributed
Did any **assessment or planning factors** contribute to or cause the adverse event? ☐ Yes ☐ No ☐ Not Known	If YES, describe what factors and how they contributed.
What **other factors** are considered relevant to the adverse event?	Describe:

Rank order the major categories of contributory factors considered responsible for the adverse event, beginning with the proximate cause, followed by the most important to less important contributory factors. If known, also include specific factors (i.e., 1a, 1b, etc.).
 	
Attach a formal Contributory Factors
	Proximate Cause:
	CF 1:
	    CF 1a:
	    CF 1b:
	    CF 1c:
	CF 2:

Diagram, if available.	CF 2a:
	CF 2b:
	CF 2c:
	CF 3:
	CF 3a:
	CF 3b:
	CF 3c:
	CF 4:
	CF 4a:
	CF 4b:
	CF 4c:
	CF 5:
	CF 5a:
	CF 5b:
	CF 5c:
	Additional Contributory Factors:

| Was a **root cause** identified?
☐ Yes   ☐ No | If YES, describe the root cause. |

RISK REDUCTION ACTIONS TAKEN – List the actions that have already been taken to reduce the risk of a future occurrence of the event under consideration. Note the date of implementation.

Description of Actions Already Taken	Date Implemented
1.	
2.	

3. 4.		

PREVENTION STRATEGIES – List from highest priority to lowest priority the recommended actions designed to prevent a future occurrence of the adverse event. Begin with a rank of 1 (highest). For each strategy or action provide an estimated cost, if known, and any additional considerations or recommendations for implementing the strategy (e.g., phase-in, immediate need, triage by risk).

Rank	STRATEGY	Estimated Cost	Special Considerations
1			
2			
3			
4			
5			

INCIDENTAL FINDINGS – List and describe any incidental findings that should be carefully reviewed for corrective action.

Describe:

APPROVAL – After review of this summary report, all team members should notify the team leader of either their approval or recommendations for revision. Following all revisions the report should be signed by the team leader prior to submission.

Signature of Team Leader:	Date Signed:

The information contained in this report is confidential and is intended solely to promote safety.

Forward this report to all RCA team members and to the following individuals:

Name	Title	Organization	Address	Email

Special Comments:

Listing of Attached Documents:

APPENDIX M
Root Cause Analysis
Executive Summary

INCIDENT: *(add summary statement – who, what, where, when.)*

CAUSES: *(Summarize primary and secondary level contributory factors and the root cause, if identified. Provide a brief statement re: the rationale for each primary factor and the root cause.)*

Contributory Factors

Factor	Rationale

Root Cause	Rationale

RECOMMENDATIONS: *(List priority recommendations and note potential effectiveness and any significant issues or special challenges that might be associated with each, i.e. pros and cons.)*

Recommendation	Estimated Effectiveness	Special Issues

Other Strategies to Consider:

INCIDENTAL FINDINGS: *(List any special incidental findings that management must be notified of along with the rationale as to why these factors increase risk.)*

Name and Title of Team Leader:

Made in the
USA
Middletown, DE